POST-MODERN USE OF THE BIBLE

EDGAR V. McKNIGHT

POST-MODERN USE OF THE BIBLE

The Emergence of Reader-Oriented Criticism

ABINGDON PRESS
Nashville

Postmodern Use of the Bible:
The Emergence of Reader-oriented Criticism

This book is printed on acid-free paper.

Library of Congress Cataloging-in-Publication Data

McKnight, Edgar V.
Postmodern use of the Bible: the emergence of reader-oriented criticism / Edgar V. McKnight.
p. cm.
Bibliography: p.
ISBN 0-687-33178-1 (pbk. : alk. paper)
1. Bible—Hermeneutics. 2. Bible—Criticism, interpretation, etc.—History—20th century. 3. Postmodernism. . Bible--Criticism, interpretation, etc.—History. I. Title.
BS476.M34 1988 88-14627
220.6—dc19 CIP

MANUFACTURED BY THE PARTHENON PRESS AT
NASHVILLE, TENNESSEE, UNITED STATES OF AMERICA

Contents

Acknowledgments

Furman University has furnished me academic challenge, opportunity, and freedom as a faculty member since 1973. President John E. Johns, the trustees, and the administration have created possibilities for effective and enjoyable learning and teaching, and my faculty colleagues and students have transformed possibility into reality. Encouragement and support for professional activities that made this book possible came from Vice President for Academic Affairs and Dean John H. Crabtree, Jr., and Furman's committees on research and faculty development. I wish to express thanks to Sandra Hack and Joyce Aldridge for assisting me as Dana Undergraduate Research Fellows in the summers of 1986 and 1987 and to Rebecca Miller and Cheryl Abernethy for typing the manuscript.

Davis Perkins began his career as Senior Editor of Academic and Reference Books at Abingdon Press with the acceptance of this manuscript. He has provided unfailingly kind and critical attention. My wife, Shirley, and my children, Lynn and Ed, have sacrificed to make it possible and pleasurable for me to carry out regular duties as a college teacher and to enjoy a career of scholarship and writing.

To Bill, George, and Cara, and to the memory of Lillian and Ralph, I dedicate this book.

Introduction

Knowledge and the Reader

Postmodernism[1] challenges an intellectual certitude that is the antithesis of freedom, faith, and imagination, but it does not support a lapse into irrationality. The postmodern attitude is akin to that recommended by John Robinson to the Pilgrims before they left for America:

> I cannot sufficiently bewail the condition of the Reformed Churches, who are come to a Period in Religion and will go at present no further than the instruments of their Reformation. The Lutheran can't be drawn to go beyond what Luther saw; whatever part of His will our God has revealed to Calvin, they will rather die than embrace it; and the Calvinists, you see, stick fast where they were left by that great man of God, who yet saw not all things. . . . I beseech you remember it is an article of your church covenant, that you be ready to receive whatever truth shall be made known to you from the written Word of God.[2]

Harry Emerson Fosdick's classic volume entitled *The Modern Use of the Bible* enabled readers in the first part of this century to make the pilgrimage into the "modern" era and to understand the Bible in an idiom informed by critical and historical assumptions and approaches. The exchange of the historical context for the dogmatic transformed biblical study into an exciting discipline both spiritually and intellectually. The critical distancing of the text in the historical approach, however, has gradually transformed biblical writings into museum pieces without contemporary relevance. For contemporary readers, a satisfying approach cannot be uncritical, but it must move beyond the critical. *Postmodern Use of the Bible* encourages a continual pilgrimage. In this book, readers are provided resources to enable them to make sense for themselves, in the light of challenges to major critical assumptions and strategies of *The Modern Use of the Bible.* The same goal is in mind—to allow the Bible to speak in a contemporary idiom.

This book is designed not only for those who, on a personal level, have become less and less satisfied with the meanings that historical criticism is capable of discerning. It is also designed for those whose retreat from history and move to relationships strictly within the text has not resulted in satisfying meaning. The book will give no comfort, however, to those who want to avoid the challenge of historical and literary criticism, for the approach is not premodern or precritical. A postmodern approach can exist only in dialogue with modern or critical assumptions and approaches. Postmodern literary study exists only in relation with historical-critical, new critical, and structural assumptions and approaches.

The postmodern perspective which allows readers to use the Bible today is that of a radical reader-oriented literary criticism, a criticism which views literature in terms of readers and their values, attitudes, and responses. This supplements and relativizes views of literature in terms of the universe imitated in the work, the author, the audience, and the work itself. A *radical* reader-oriented criticism is postmodern in that it challenges the critical assumption that a disinterested reader can approach a text objectively and obtain verifiable knowledge by applying certain scientific strategies. A radical reader-oriented approach sees the strategies, the criteria for criticism and verification, the "information" obtained by the process, and the use made of such "information" in light of the reader. The reader is no more autonomous than the text in postmodernism; the reader and the text are interdependent. The text is actualized by the reader in a fashion that the text may be said to actualize the reader.

The beginning of the emphasis on the reader in American literary criticism did not give evidence of the *radical* conclusions to be reached.[3] In the beginning, the effort was directed toward giving proper attention to the temporal dimension of the act of reading. The New Criticism (which was the background for development of reader-response criticism) had emphasized the text itself and had developed procedures for careful analysis of the text. The intentions of the author did not give direction in New Criticism because these intentions were judged to be unavailable. On the other hand, the responses of the reader were too variable to give direction. Attention to the text itself revolutionized earlier biographical and historical emphases, but as New Criticism began to exhaust its potentiality, *reading* and the response of readers gained vitality.

New Criticism's suspicion of the variability of readers' responses continued in early reader-response criticism. To maintain a concept of validity, different levels of experience in reading were distinguished: a primary level, shared by all readers regardless of differences in education and culture, and a secondary level, which could be seen as a reaction (emotional or intellectual) to the experience of the primary level. The proper practice of literary criticism involved the suppression of the subjective and idiosyncratic secondary level in favor of the response shared by all readers.

But how could proper responses be distinguished from improper ones? Only on the basis of an object (the text) in relation to which readers' experiences could be tested. The integrity of the text was thus retained in order to claim universality and objectivity for a reader-response approach. The radical departure from New Critical assumptions came when it was discerned that literature is a conventional category dependent on subjective perception. This involves the denial of a basic, or neutral, language of literature unrelated to the perception and response of the reader.

A radical reader-response approach may be evaded temporarily by defining the reader as a member of a community, which determines the attention given by the reader and the kind of responses made by the reader. This emphasis on the community allows proper readings to be identified; proper readings are those in agreement with the beliefs and practices of the community of readers. The business of criticism, then, may be seen as the determination of the perspective from which reading will proceed, and the validation of readings is accomplished by demonstration that readings are consistent with the interpretative community. But since such perspectives differ, criticism may come to consist of persuasion that the interests and the tacitly-understood goals of one group are superior to those of another group. A radical reader-oriented criticism neither denies the influence of the community on the individual, nor attempts to validate readings on the basis of community goals and interests. It stresses the role of the individual reader in the process of making sense. Otherwise the "sense" made of the text and the "idiom" into which the text is translated are not that of the reader but that of an external authority.

When criticism questioned the status of the language of literature, the knowledge involved in literature, and the nature of the self or the subject in the reading process, a revolution took place. Thrust squarely into the field of literature were the philosophical questioning of the intrinsic limits of knowledge (epistemology) and the reaction to such questioning by movements such as hermeneutics, structuralism, and poststructuralism, and phenomenology.[4] Parallel to the conclusion of reader-response criticism that there is no absolutely neutral language of literature to serve as a foundation for readers' responses is the conclusion of philosophy that there is no absolute foundation that can be used in the determination of knowledge. The foundationalist approach in philosophy would assume the possibility of advancing a proposition whose truth is demonstrable without any sort of assumptions and from which further theories could be strictly developed. In place of such a foundationalist theory of knowledge came a circular theory, whereby knowledge is justified in nonlinear, or circular, fashion through the relationship of the results obtained to the beginning point.

In literature, this circular approach can be observed in the relationship of the meaning of a word to the meaning of the sentence in which the word is used. The meaning of the sentence depends on the meanings of the words. The meanings of the words, however, cannot be determined apart from the meaning of the sentences. There is a mutual "causality." But the sentence in turn, is embedded in a larger linguistic and literary unit that determines the meaning of its sentence, and literature as a system is related to nonliterary systems. So literature (as philosophy) is not only circular, but it also consists of a circle of circles. Knowledge and literature as circles of circles do not exist in a vacuum; they exist in relation to life. Thought is not sovereign; it depends on the being of life and experience (ontology).

The limits of knowledge and the failure to establish some final foundation for knowledge have been applied in a dramatic fashion in literature in the skeptical deconstruction associated with Jacques Derrida. Skepticism, however, is not the only possible conclusion. Skepticism results from the assumption that foundationalism is the only route to knowledge, or that the only kind of knowledge that counts is that which is based on foundationalism. A reader-oriented approach results from the assumption that knowledge (epistemology) is always related to life (ontology) and that the only sort of knowledge that really counts is knowledge grounded in life.

Reader-response criticism has been directly influenced by fields of study intimately related both to textual interpretation and to the epistemological revolution. These include hermeneutics, structuralism and poststructuralism, and phenomenology. Long before the advent of reader-response criticism on the American scene, hermeneutics transformed the question of interpretation into the question of knowledge ("How do we know?") and the question of being ("What is the mode of being of that being who only exists through understanding?"). Rudolf Bultmann and the New Hermeneutic utilized the relationship between being, language, and humankind postulated by Martin Heidegger. The New Hermeneutic was unable to establish a satisfying coordination between the role and function of the Bible, the language of the Bible, and specific strategies designed to allow the biblical text to carry out the postulated role. As a result, the hermeneutical tradition in biblical studies stagnated. Some forms of reader-response criticism, however, move back to the idea of Heidegger, that the understanding of a text does not simply involve the discovery of an inner meaning contained in the text, that to understand a text is to unfold the possibility of being, which is indicated by that text.

The structural tradition has also become important for reader-response criticism. The literary structuralism that became known to Americans in the 1960s and 1970s was French structuralism with its emphasis on order and necessity, rather than human choice and freedom—factors emphasized by existentialism, which was the background for French structuralism. In poststructural developments associated with Derrida, order is replaced with a radical disordering. The opposition between French structuralism and poststructuralism or deconstruction is actually mediated in the broader structural tradition, which integrates the structural view of a work with history and the individual. In this structuralist tradition, literature is a system standing in correlation with other systems that help to define literature. Literature in general and specific works of literature, therefore, are influenced by changes in culture. A dialectical relationship also exists between the individual and culture. The individual may be seen either as defined by culture or as the subject and ultimate source of aesthetic interaction. In a radical reader-oriented approach, the reader is no longer an irrelevant individual, superimposing private associations onto a social meaning, but an active force who is indispensable to meaning from the beginning.

The phenomenological tradition conceives of the literary work of art in such a way as to emphasize the role of the individual reader. The work of art itself is distinguished from the work as an aesthetic object that is constituted or actualized through the intentional act of reading. The complexity of a literary work and its apprehension are such that readers cannot give themselves equally to all of the components of the total apprehension. Only a few of the multiplicity of experienced and interwoven acts become central. The rest are only co-experienced. This means that there is constant change with regard to which component acts are central at any particular moment. The same literary work is apprehended, then, in various changing "aspects."

This book is organized like an hourglass. The first two chapters form the upper part of the hourglass and examine the essential structure of precritical and critical approaches. Systems of language and literature are shown to be related to other systems that allow readers to translate biblical language into an understandable idiom. The dogmatic approach of the ancient and medieval church, historical criticism, Bultmann's existential hermeneutics, and contemporary literary approaches are related to world views that influence the role and function of biblical literature and the strategies that enable that role and function to be carried out. The first chapter reexamines the history of biblical criticism as a continuing dialogue between world views and interpretative strategies. The precritical hermeneutics of the ancient and medieval church operated on a metonymic function of language; words stood for something else, be it ideas, thoughts, or a transcendental order. Critical hermeneutics since the Enlightenment has viewed language as being descriptive of a natural, temporal order. Words no longer required to be interpreted in the light of an order beyond the visible world of phenomena, but within a spatially and temporally limited world. The change from precritical to critical hermeneutics did not entail a substantial change in method, but rather an alteration of the referential viewpoint.

The second chapter examines contemporary interpretative strategies that operate in tandem with the historical-critical approach. History-like application has been followed in the case of movements called "progressive revelation" and "biblical theology." Canonical criticism, the *new* biblical theology associated with Peter Stuhlmacher at the University of Tübingen, and sociological exegesis either redefine historical method or change the focus of critical attention. Theologians have distinguished between historical criticism and study of the Bible as scripture or canon in such a way that historical-critical study is maintained, but the results are not viewed as the basis for theology. These quasi-historical strategies illustrate both the lack of contemporary satisfaction with historical criticism *per se* and the power of the historical-critical paradigm. History-like and theological-historical approaches are constrained by the critical world view with its model of language. The lack of contemporary satisfaction with conventional historical-critical approaches is evidence of an alteration in world view and the need for another model of language. An approach to the Bible as literature from the perspective of the epistemological revolution may do justice to the biblical text and to the needs of contemporary readers.

The central, third, chapter delineates the motifs and movements in contemporary literary studies, influenced by the structuralist-formalist revolution. This revolution may be perceived as an application in language and literature of the antifoundationalist insight. In the structural tradition, phenomena are understood in terms of relationships at a given point of time, instead of in terms of origin or evolution. Meaning, therefore, is no longer seen in terms of an original "cause" or ultimate "effect" but in terms of relationship. This structuralist-formalist perception has transformed the study of all cultural phenomena, but it has become particularly important in the study of literature. Changes take place in various phenomena over time, of course, but the meaning of the alterations is related to the modification that takes place in the various structures or sets of relationships from one epoch to another. The reader-oriented literary criticism resulting from structuralist-formalist insights stresses the dynamic interaction between the text and the reader in the process of reading. It also emphasizes the role of the reader in actualizing systems or factors impinging the text and textual interpretation.

The fourth and fifth chapters (the bottom of the hourglass) show how a reader may make sense of the Bible in a way to be faithful to contemporary theory and, therefore, to the reader's own competence and need. The approach may be described as a hermeneutic or reader-oriented literary approach. The fourth chapter suggests how contemporary readers may conceptualize the totality of the Bible as literature. The role and function of the Bible as literature are related to the role of literature as a whole in that literature enables readers to make sense of their world. Biblical literature, however, enables readers to make sense of their world as a "given" rather than as the result of human ingenuity and achievement. The sacred (which is methodologically excluded with the critical paradigm because of its need for data that can be tested by extrinsic correspondence) may be imaged by contemporary readers who acknowledge the place of life and experience in the discovery and validation of knowledge. The work of John Macquarrie, in particular, is used to show readers how the sacred may be reimaged. The chapter suggests that we may be moving into a postcritical use of language that is somewhat parallel to a precritical poetic or metaphorical phase of language in which there is not a division between subject and object, humankind and nature—a division necessary for the critical approach. Macquarrie's appropriation of Heidegger introduces a concept of language as known in the revelatory experience, bringing new understanding both of oneself and of the wider being within which one has life. We may be reverting to the metaphorical language of the biblical communities, to a reading of biblical texts as words of power.

The fifth chapter explicates critical and hermeneutical processes by which sense is made of texts and by which texts affect readers. The basic activity is that of determining relationships (structures) of lower-level linguistic and literary elements in the light of higher-level schemata (formal and thematic). The words of a sentence, for example, may be related in appropriate fashion in the light of linguistic conventions that govern the structure of sentences and in the light of some theme that constrains verbal meaning. Lower-level elements are always related to higher-level schemata, which depend on still higher-level schemata. At the end of the process (in the view of reader-oriented assumptions) are life and lived experience. This experience, in fact, operates at the very lowest level. It is on the basis of experience that preliminary guesses are made in the process of reading, to be confirmed or modified at later stages of the process.

A reader-oriented literary approach will begin with the view of the role and function of the Bible, explicated earlier—that is, the Bible will not be approached as "scientific" writing to be reduced to scientific codes. The actualization of genres, the determination of the "ideas" of the individual books, and so on will be influenced by the literary role, just as Augustine's treatment of textual questions was governed by the role of the Bible in enabling readers to love God and to love neighbor.

Notes

1. The term *postmodern* is useful because of its imprecision and convoluted logic. In a formal sense, the *post*modern is an "advance" beyond the modern, but postmodernism is not merely a new movement that has succeeded modernism. A dialectical relationship exists between the modern and postmodern; the postmodern "advance" utilizes the assumptions and strategies of the modern in order to challenge them.

Postmodernism assumes different forms because of different expressions of modernism. Shailer Matthews, author of *The Faith of Modernism* (New York: Macmillan, 1924), defined modernism in religion as "the use of the methods of modern science to find, state and use the permanent and central values of inherited orthodoxy in meeting the needs of a modern world" (p. 23). The traditional order (inherited orthodoxy) was severely altered by the natural, social, and historical sciences. In literature, modernism represented a break with traditional forms and techniques. But it, too, remained concerned with order, albeit an order created within the works of literature themselves. In religion and literature, postmodernism represents a break with the modernist revision of an earlier order.

2. Daniel Neal, *History of the Puritans,* part 2, chap. 2. Quoted in Ernest A. Payne, *The Fellowship of Believers* (London: The Cary Kingsgate Press, 1952), p. 74.

3. See Stanley Fish, *Is There a Text in This Class? The Authority of Interpretative Communities* (Cambridge, Mass: Harvard University Press, 1982), pp. 1-17, for a sketch of developments in reader-response criticism.

4. See Tom Rockmore, *Hegel's Circular Epistemology,* (Bloomington: Indiana University Press, 1986), pp. 159-75, for a summary of recent developments in phenomenology and analytic thought in the light of an antifoundationalist theory of knowledge.

Chapter One

How Have We Made Sense of the Bible?

Precritical and Critical Uses from a Postmodern Perspective

The precritical dogmatic use of the Bible is most often seen as an essentially wrong-headed method that is responsible for all sorts of biblical misunderstandings and theological errors. At its best, it is seen as a necessary stage on the way to more enlightened approaches, such as historical or existential interpretation. From a postmodern and structural perspective, the dogmatic method is not greatly different from later methods. All of these methods are entirely consistent with the prevailing view of the world and with methods authenticated by that worldview.

Proof of the validity of a particular method may be offered, of course, but such proof consists of statements that gain their value as evidence because they are consistent with the prevailing view of the world which provides the method to begin with. Historical critics' justification for seeking the setting in life of the forms of the tradition, for example, is the assumption that the meaning of the forms grow out of the historical and sociological circumstances of their origin. Rudolf Bultmann's conviction that biblical myth is to be studied to discover the way we understand ourselves in the world depends on his assumptions that in "all interpretation which has comprehension as its basis, the presupposition for understanding is the interpreter's relationship in his life to the subject which is directly expressed in the text" and that "inquiry into the reality of human existence is inquiry about God and the manifestations of God."[1]

The traditional way of presenting the different methods of study is essentially a validation of whatever happens to be the contemporary method.[2] Earlier approaches are arranged in a sequence (historical and/or logical) that leads naturally to the current method. The dogmatic approach of the ancient and medieval church, with its allegorical strategy, is seen as superseded by the historical-critical approach of the Enlightenment. Then, the historical-critical approach is either seen as authenticating a variety of contemporary approaches—ranging from the existential hermeneutics of the Bultmann school to current canonical and sociological exegesis—or as being superseded by nonhistorical approaches, which emphasize synchronic structures and relationships (relationships within the text itself and between the text and extratextual factors at one particular period), rather than diachronic or historical relationships.

Is it possible to break out of such a system? Not in any absolute sense. The discussion of approaches in this chapter, for example, is influenced by the presupposition that meaning is not simply a result of diachronic relationships but is also a product of synchronic relationships. The assumption that a variety of coexisting and dynamically interdependent factors is involved in interpretation enables us to identify at least some of these factors in earlier epochs and to determine which factors were most influential in those epochs.

This chapter will begin with the approach of the ancient and medieval church as exemplified by Augustine and against that background will discuss historical and existential approaches.

The Dogmatic Method of the Ancient and Medieval Church

A reexamination of the dogmatic method from a contemporary perspective demonstrates the interdependence of a variety of factors in the effort to make sense of the Bible. Some of these factors were known, acknowledged, and discussed by the ancient and medieval church. However, some were part-and-parcel of the prevailing world view and of methods supplied and validated by that world view. We are able to see those at-least-partially unconscious presuppositions and factors clearly today because they are foreign to our world view.

For the purpose of this work, the approach of the ancient and medieval church will be considered as a unity, and the system of interpretation explicated by Augustine will serve as exemplary of the entire period. It is clear that within this broad unity, development and variation existed, but Augustine is an appropriate example for the entire period because he restated an ecclesiastical system that had been developed by earlier church leaders, such as Origen and Tertullian, and Augustine's famous treatise *On Christian Doctrine* was the most influential text on exposition for the medieval church.

Factors in the Dogmatic Approach

The best-known aspect of early Christian interpretation is allegory. By this means, Augustine is able to find Christian meaning throughout the Old Testament. The flood, for example, is a sacramental sign for Augustine. It figures salvation, the cross, and the Church.

> Under the sacramental sign of the flood, however, in which the righteous were rescued by the wood, there was also a fore-announcement of the Church which was to be, which Christ, its King and God, has raised on high, by the mystery of His cross, in safety from the submersion of this world.[3]

The "allegorical art" of Augustine reaches its most "rarefied heights" in his interpretation of the parable of the good Samaritan.

> *A certain man went down from Jerusalem to Jericho;* Adam himself is meant; *Jerusalem* is the heavenly city of peace, from whose blessedness Adam fell; *Jericho* means the moon and signifies our mortality, because it is born, waxes, wanes, and dies. *Thieves* are the devil and his angels. *Who stripped him,* namely of his immortality; *and beat him,* by persuading him to sin; *and left him half-dead,* because in so far as man can understand and know God, he lives, but in so far as he is wasted and oppressed by sin, he is dead; he is therefore called *half-dead.*[4]

How was it possible for the Old Testament story of the flood and the simple story of the good Samaritan to mean so much for Augustine? It is evident that factors or systems beyond the words on the page were involved.

The Church and the Canon. One important factor in the ancient and medieval system of interpretation, of course, is the church. Scripture is to be understood within the church. The appeal to the Church as the guarantor of the scriptures, which Augustine expressed in a letter to his friend Honoratus, is typical: "From whom did I derive my faith in Christ? . . . I see that I owe my faith to opinion and report widely spread and firmly established among the peoples and nations of the earth and that those people everywhere observe the mysteries of the Catholic Church."[5] The movement, however, is not seen by Augustine as a simple move from the Church of his own day and its dogma to the exposition of the scriptures, for the Church Augustine envisions is that portrayed in the scripture as the people of God whose history moves from Adam until the day of judgment. The church, for Augustine, is "the Church spread out through time and rooted in eternity, proclaimed in the prophets, established in the Incarnation and teaching of Christ, and today to be seen in the universal Church."[6] Nevertheless "the most important feature of Augustine's biblical exegesis," Gerald Bonner notes, "is its ecclesial quality. The Bible must be read and understood within the framework of the life and doctrine of the Christian community and not interpreted by mere private judgment, however learned."[7]

The Reader. The critical capacity and need of the individual reader are also factors that must be utilized and satisfied. Augustine had no doubt as to the potentiality of human reason, at least to the point of mastering the rules of biblical interpretation expounded in the treatise *On Christian Doctrine*. The work was proposed with the view that "the man who is in possession of the rules which I here attempt to lay down, if he meet with an obscure passage in the books which he reads, will not need an interpreter to lay open the secret to him."[8] In his dealings with his former co-religionists, the Manichees, Augustine explicated the relationship of reason and authority. Manichaeism represented itself as rational and saw the Catholics as irrational authoritarians. Augustine recognized the need for authority to direct human understanding, but did not reject the power of reason. The dialectical relationship between authority and reason in biblical understanding was stated in an appeal to a correspondent to cherish the intellect, "For the Holy Scriptures themselves which persuade us to have faith in great matters before we understand them, cannot be useful to you unless you rightly understand them."[9]

The Enjoyment of God. The broadest context for the interpretation and exposition of scripture is the enjoyment of God. This context, indeed, relativizes critical activity of the interpreter and subsidiary roles and functions of scripture. The importance of this context is evidenced from its treatment in the first book of *On Christian Doctrine.* A distinction is made, first of all, between signs and things and then between things to be used and things to be enjoyed. A sign signifies what it causes to come into someone's mind as a consequence of itself; words are signs. A thing differs from a sign in that a thing is something in itself, not used as a sign of something else. Things, however, may either be used (like signs) or enjoyed: "To use [a thing] is to employ whatever means are at one's disposal to obtain what one desires." To enjoy a thing, on the other hand, is to "rest with satisfaction in it for its own sake" (*OCD*, 1.4.4). For Christians, then, signs and things to be used function in relation to higher realities, in relation to objects for enjoyment. For Christians, "the true objects of enjoyment . . . are the Father and the Son and the Holy Spirit"(1.5.5). The scriptures are not on a par with these things to be enjoyed. They are to be used in relation to these things. "The end of the Law, and of all Holy Scripture, is the love of an object which is to be enjoyed, and the love of an object which can enjoy that other in fellowship with ourselves" (1.35.39).

Since the love of God and of neighbor is the end of scripture, Augustine declares that the purpose of a biblical text can be reached even when the meaning drawn from that text is not "the precise meaning which the author . . . intended to express in that place" (1.36.40). If a mistake in interpretation tends to build up love, in Augustine's opinion, the interpreter "goes astray in much the same way as a man who by mistake quits the high road, but yet reaches through the fields the same place to which the road leads" (1.36.41). The primacy of enjoyment of God and the love of God and neighbor relativize even such matters as textual criticism and translation. So long as no theological difficulties are raised, Augustine will accept variant readings without attempting to discriminate between them. The reading of Romans 5:14: "Death reigned from Adam until Moses, even over them that sinned in the likeness of Adam's transgression" (in place of the more usual "had not sinned") accords well with the doctrine that all men sinned in Adam. Therefore, Augustine feels no need to pursue the matter further. Both readings are acceptable because they conform to the Catholic doctrine (see *Letters,* 157,3.19). The translations of Isaiah 7:9 "If ye will not believe, ye shall not understand" and "If ye will not believe, ye shall not abide" each contain "a great truth" for "those who read with knowledge" (*OCD,* 2.12.17). Even the scriptures themselves are dispensable in that they are not needed by "a man who is resting upon faith, hope and love, and who keeps a firm hold upon these . . . except for the purpose of instructing others" (*OCD,* 1.39.43).

Language. As an instrument to serve the enjoyment of God, the scriptures function as conventional signs. "Conventional signs . . . are those which living beings mutually exchange for the purpose of showing, as well as they can, the feelings of their minds, or their perceptions, or their thoughts" (*OCD,* 2.2.3). Augustine indicates that in reading holy scripture "men seek nothing more than to find out the thought and will of those by whom it was written" but through this process, men may seek "to find out the will of God, in accordance with which they believe these men to have spoken" (*OCD,* 2.5.6).

The conventional nature of signs in the holy scriptures means that attention must be given to all of the linguistic, literary, and other resources that humans use in communication. Augustine acknowledges not only the value of the knowledge of the biblical languages, but also the value of various kinds of knowledge offered outside the church, those which are not a "mere human invention" (*OCD*, 2.27.41). The "historical importance" of *On Christian Doctrine* is even noted by Gerald Bonner as being the "justification which it supplied for the reading by Christians of pagan literature."[10]

Neoplatonism and the Reality to Which All Signs Refer. To suggest that more is involved for the "properly prepared" reader than the ordinary deciphering of signs, Augustine develops an analogy from the story of the Exodus. In the analogy, profane learning, the conventional use of signs, and the ultimate referent of all signs are related. The properly prepared student of holy scripture "will feel that, whatever may be the riches he brings with him out of Egypt . . . unless he has kept the passover, he cannot be safe. Now Christ is our passover" (*OCD*, 2.41.62). He also states that "the liberty that comes by Christ took those whom it found under bondage to useful signs . . . and, interpreting the signs to which they were in bondage, set them free by raising them to the realities of which these were signs" (*OCD*, 3.8.12).

It is only by going beyond the sign that is seen and temporal to that reality to which all signs refer that one is spiritual and free. The vision of the relationship of conventional signs to an ultimate reality "to which all such signs refer" (*OCD*, 3.9.13) does not simply develop from an application of the tools of language and literature to the biblical text. It is due in part to the world view of Augustine's day. For Augustine, biblical interpretation and meaning had to cohere with the philosophical and theological system of thought that saw the visible world of phenomena as an exteriorization, an imperfect imitation of the intelligible world. The properly prepared student, who is spiritual and free, will look beyond the sensible phenomena to the realities they express since, as a modern student of Augustine says, the Neoplatonic conceptualization was "as basic to the thought of the age of Augustine as is the idea of Evolution to our own."[11]

The Platonic and Neoplatonic understanding of language is, of course, historically conditioned. It is most often seen, and found wanting, in relation to the critical descriptive understanding of language developed during the Enlightenment, but it must also be seen in the light of an earlier poetic or "hieroglyphic" stage of language. In this poetic stage, subject and object are not clearly separated but are linked by a common power or energy, which may be brought into being by the articulating of words. The stage of language that was operative in the ancient and medieval church began with Plato and continued to the sixteenth century. In this stage words become essentially the outward expression of inner ideas or thoughts.

> The basis of expression here is moving from the metaphorical, with its sense of identity of life or power or energy between man and nature ("this is that"), to a relationship that is rather metonymic ("that is put for that"). Specifically, words are "put for" thoughts, and are the outward expressions of an inner reality. But this reality is not merely "inside." Thoughts indicate the existence of a transcendent order "above," which only thinking can communicate with and which only words can express. Thus metonymic language is, or tends to become, analogical language, a verbal imitation of a reality beyond itself that can be conveyed most directly by words. [12]

The dependence of Augustine's system on a Neoplatonic conceptualization that did not come from the Bible and the church would not have called his system into question, for, in Augustine's opinion, the teachings of the Neoplatonists are like those riches brought out of Egypt. They ought to be claimed by Christians "for our own use from those who have unlawful possession of it." The truths of Neoplatonism are like "gold and silver, which they did not create themselves, but dug out of the mines of God's providence which are everywhere scattered abroad." When the Christian "separates himself in spirit from the miserable fellowship of these men," he ought to take the truths they discovered and devote them "to their proper use in preaching the Gospel" (*OCD,* 2.40.60).

Dogmatic Biblical Exegesis

Epistemological Foundation. The epistemological ideas that served as the foundation of aesthetic thought and interpretation of the Middle Ages may be stated in an abstract form.

> We cannot perceive the truth by analyzing separate individual phenomena—individual phenomena stem from certain true, general categories which are given beforehand. Cognition proceeds through equating these individual phenomena with general categories which are conceived of as primary. The act of cognition does not consist in the revelation of the individual or the specific, but in the process of abstraction from the particular, raising it to the general, and in the end, to the universal.[13]

Augustine, of course, did not think in an abstract way about the "universal." He saw the Bible in relation to God. The Bible for Augustine, then, could be seen as the result of the linguistic and literary tools of the human creature, but it must also be seen as a sign of God, a communication intrinsically far above the pitch of human minds but available as a sign. The attitude of Augustine is natural, according to Peter Brown, "once it is thought possible for something larger than our conscious awareness to be capable of active communication, whether this be the 'whole' personality, conscious and unconscious of the modern psychoanalyst, or the ineffable 'Word' of the Early Christian exegete."[14]

The Basic Procedure. Brown summarizes the basic procedure of biblical exegesis in such a context.

> The exegete, therefore, faced with the Bible conceived of as a communication of this kind, will train himself to listen for the single, hidden "will" that had expressed itself in the deliberate selection of every word of the text: for in a sacred text, "everything was said exactly as it needed to be said." Thus the first question he must ask is not "what," "what was the exact nature of this particular religious practice in the ancient Near East?" but "*why*"—"why does this incident, this word and no other, occur at just this moment in the interminable monologue of God; and so, what aspect of His deeper message does it communicate? Like the child who asked the basic question: "Mummy, *why* is a cow?" Augustine will run through the text of the Bible in such a way that every sermon is punctuated by "*Quare . . . Quare . . . Quare*" "Why? . . . Why? . . . Why?"[15]

The Allegorical Approach. The allegorical method must be seen as an integral part of the system of making sense of the world and of biblical texts in the framework of Neoplatonic thought basic for the world of Augustine. Since the end of the text, the *why?* of the text, is the "love to God for His own sake" and "love to one's self and one's neighbor for God's sake," a rule for interpretation is offered by Augustine: "To carefully turn over in our minds and meditate upon what we read till an interpretation be found that tends to establish the reign of love" (*OCD,* 3.15.23). A reading that uses signs in a purely conventional fashion may establish an appropriate meaning for many texts, but not for all texts. Augustine gives a principle to be applied in such cases: "Whatever there is in the word of God that cannot, when taken literally, be referred either to purity of life or soundness of doctrine, you may set down as figurative. Purity of life has reference to the love of God and one's neighbor; soundness of doctrine to the knowledge of God and one's neighbor" (*OCD,* 3.10.14). The coherence of the theologically explained universe and the allegorical method was so self-evident and compelling in the medieval period that even such an original vernacular poet of the fourteenth century as Dante expected his *Divine Comedy* to be interpreted within that system.[16]

The Function of Allegory. The need to unravel the mystery of the symbol in the allegorical approach stimulated the mind by incongruity and shock, and the reader gained pleasure by lingering in symbols. Augustine himself acknowledged a delight in the use of biblical figures. In *On Christian Doctrine,* he cites Song of Solomon 4:2

> Your teeth are like a flock of shorn ewes
> that have come up from the washing, whereof every one bears twins, and none is barren among them

as praise of the Church under the figure of a beautiful woman. He acknowledges that the hearer learns no more from the figure than from plain language.

> And yet . . . I feel greater pleasure in contemplating holy men, when I view them as the teeth of the Church, tearing men away from their errors, and bringing them into the Church's body, with all their harshness softened down, just as if they had been torn off and masticated by the teeth. . . . But why I view them with greater delight under that aspect than if no such figure were drawn from the sacred books, though the fact would remain the same and the knowledge the same, is another question, and one very difficult to answer. Nobody, however, has any doubt about the facts, both that it is pleasanter in some cases to have knowledge communicated through figures, and that what is attended with difficulty in the seeking gives greater pleasure in the finding. (*OCD*, 2.6.7-8)

Augustine, however, does not see the pleasure involved in the deciphering of figures as an end in itself. He sees the plain passages as designed "to satisfy our hunger" and the more obscure "to stimulate our appetite" (*OCD*, 2.6.8).

Historical Aspects. The ecclesial system of Augustine did not ignore the historical content and context of the scriptures emphasized by later historical criticism. It relativized them or accommodated them to a different value or significance than did historical criticism. Historical events that were questionable ethically were accommodated to the dogmatic standards by Augustine in various ways, depending on the nature of the historical events. Apparently wicked actions of holy men, and even of

God, could be rationalized by explaining the acts in the light of circumstances prevailing in an earlier epoch. Polygamy, for example, was necessary in an earlier period in order to assure numerous offspring. A woman's relationship with several husbands could not be rationalized, however, because the woman would not become more fruitful as a result. "In regard to matters of this sort, whatever the holy men of those times did without lust, scripture passes over without blame, although they did things which could not be done at the present time, except through lust" (*OCD*, 3.12.20). Actions or sayings that could not be so rationalized, that must be considered wicked under any circumstances, are to be seen as "wholly figurative, and the hidden kernel of meaning they contain is to be picked out as food for the nourishment of charity" (*OCD*, 3.12.18). The historical narratives, whether looked upon as reporting actual events that create no ethical problems, as reporting events that are blameless from an earlier perspective, are as wholly figurative, are to be interpreted as "bearing ultimately upon the end of love toward God or our neighbor, or both" (*OCD*, 3.12.20).

The historical origin and nature of biblical books, the fact that the books resulted from authors in historically defined times and places, is not ignored by Augustine. He refers repeatedly to biblical authors and meanings they intended (see *OCD*, 1.36.40; 1.32.41; 2.2.3), and he discusses questions of authorship and dating of biblical books. Augustine is also aware that scripture is the record of human history as well as the record of divine action, and Augustine has been credited with giving a far greater significance to the temporal and historical than did the Neoplatonists. It has even been suggested that in this respect "Augustine represents a decisive factor in the history of Western biblical exegesis."[17] Clearly the distinction between the ancient and medieval church and the church following the Enlightenment was not essentially between awareness and lack of awareness of the historical aspects of the scriptures. It was over the locus of meaning.

The Dogmatic Approach as Paradigm

The views of self, world, text, language, and meaning have changed since Augustine's day. If the concept of language from Plato to the sixteenth century was *metonymic* (in that words are "put for" thoughts and are outward expressions of an inner reality), the concept of language that became dominant in the Enlightenment was descriptive. Language is treated as primarily description of an objective natural order.

> The ideal to be achieved by words is framed on the model of truth by correspondence. A verbal structure is set up beside what it describes, and is called "true" if it seems to provide a satisfactory correspondence to it. The criterion of truth is related to the external source of the description rather than to the inner consistency of the argument.[18]

The critical capacity of the interpreter, necessary for the determination of truth with such a view of language, became central in the Enlightenment and continued unchallenged up to the developments in psychology that make the idea of an autonomous "self" untenable. The world and the text as objects of dispassionate study by critics remained a viable concept until the values inherited from the Middle Ages (serving as the horizon for critical investigation) were eaten away by Cartesian rationality itself. Just as the world gradually acquired a foreboding ambiguity (with truth composed of a multitude of relative truths), the truth of the text became relativized. The concept of language as merely an instrument for human intercourse has altered. Language has assumed a position transcendent to humanity, text, and all cultural expressions. Language, for example, has been seen as a schema, determining the way cultural phenomena and even humankind itself are perceived. This elevation of the concept of language from tool to master has modified the concept of humankind, world, text, and meaning.

In spite of the changing perspectives of the factors in interpretation and their relationship to each other, the methods of interpretation since the dissolution of the dogmatic approach have followed the same formal procedure as that of the ancient and medieval church. The same factors are involved: a text that consists of conventional signs, agreement on the nature of the referent of the text (what the text is about at the most abstract or ultimate level), and satisfying and appropriate linguistic and literary tools and methods to extract the agreed upon significance. As we have observed, the view of the nature of the reader (or readership) and the world in which the reader makes sense of biblical texts are as important for interpretation as the text itself. Changing perspectives of the reader and the reader's world have altered dramatically, and these alterations have changed the perspectives on the nature of the biblical text, the nature of its meaning, and appropriate strategies for interpretation.

The Historical-Critical Method

The historical approach does precisely what the allegorical approach did: It enables the reader, or readership, to find expected and satisfying meaning in the text. At a formal level, then, precisely the same method is being followed: A reader is establishing coherence between the world and the text. The difference, however, is that the theological universe of the ancient and medieval world was radically altered in the period of the Enlightenment. The altered method of interpretation is not the result of a gradual refinement of method or discovery of new resources to assist method. It is the result of a new world, which demanded new methods of accommodation.

Factors in the Historical Approach

The Critical Spirit. A new conception of the world emerged from the Renaissance and Reformation. The recovery of classical texts and the liberation of the literature from the anti-pagan distrust of the literary imagination in the Renaissance were followed by the Reformation, whose leaders sided with those who upheld the right of private judgment as opposed to externally imposed authority. The new spirit that had come into Western life and thought emphasized reason and criticism over against authority, and the mode of criticism that came to be the "self-evident" correct mode in biblical study was the historical-critical. Often the terms *historical* or *critical* alone are used because of the assumption that the critical method had to be the historical. In fact, however, *critical* does not necessarily mean *historical*. The *historical-critical* method is, in fact, supported by postulates related to human critical capacity *and* to the locus and criterion of meaning. The basic postulate is that of human reason and the supremacy of reason as the ultimate criterion for truth. Descartes may be credited with the most influential formulation of this idea and the introduction of the new mentality that was to become an attitude of mind in religious as well as scientific matters. The human mind is capable of attaining truth concerning the general nature of the world and does so by the method of doubt, rejecting accepted ideas and opinions until they have been established by self-evident facts.[19]

Historicality of Literary Documents. The historical method did not simply develop from a new attitude toward humanity's critical capacity and the successful application of reason in the study of the material world. Nevertheless it did become the accepted critical method in the human sciences in the nineteenth century. The successful approach to the material world on the basis of reason and scientific principles consistent with the data of the world led to the conclusion that the human sciences were also susceptible to being investigated critically and scientifically. The framework for making sense of the human world could obviously no longer be that provided by the Neoplatonists, but what could replace that framework? The historicality of literary documents and of other cultural phenomena replaced the framework provided by the theological conceptualization of the ancient and medieval world. That is, the cultural documents and artifacts are bound up not with a pre-existing world, of which the artifacts are an exteriorization. They are to be understood precisely within the temporally and spatially limited context of their origins.

Accompanying the emphasis on the historicality of the phenomena was the insight into historical process and the awareness of the emergence of novelty. The scientific principle of evolution and the idea of progress, then, went hand in hand with the development of the historical method in the nineteenth century. A particular event is to be understood in its place in a chain of events proceeding in a cause and effect relationship. This principle of *correlation* is one of the three interrelated principles on which historical inquiry rests. The historical cycles of human life influence and intersect one another in such a way that a change at any one point in the historical nexus effects a change in the entire set of relationships. Ernst Troeltsch declared that "the sole task of history in its specifically theoretical aspect is to explain every movement, process, state, and nexus of things by reference to the web of its causal relations." He discerned that the development of the historical-critical explanation of cause presupposed a revolution in the consciousness of the West.

> The causal explanation of all that happens, the setting of the individual life in its true relations, the interpretation of events in their most intricate interaction, the placing of mankind in a rounded system of ceaseless change—these constitute the essential function and result of modern historical reflection. The latter, viewed as a whole, forms a new scientific mode of representing man and his development, and, as such, shows at all points an absolute contrast to the Biblico-theological views of later antiquity.[20]

Two additional principles or assumptions are necessary for the scientific historical approach. The principle of *criticism* affirms that judgments about the past are not to be classified simply as true or false but are to be seen as claiming only a greater or lesser degree of probability. Historical judgments are always open to revision. The principle of *analogy* affirms that humans are able to make such judgments of probability only by presupposing that their own present experience is similar to the experience of people of past epochs.[21] By the nineteenth century, the assumptions of the historical method had penetrated so deeply into Western consciousness that it was impossible even to think about the assumptions. These had become "a part of the furniture" of Western mentality.[22]

What was present but inert in the ancient and medieval church—awareness of historically constrained authors and meanings of biblical writings and the historical nature of the events narrated—became the active theme in the historical-critical method. Readers examined historical narratives as sources for the historical events they recounted, and the teaching of the various writings were examined in the light of the historical contexts of the writings themselves. Biblical passages were given their full historical weight and not simply explicated as exteriorizations of the intelligible world, as phenomena that could even be unrelated to historical context through allegorical interpretation. The historical approach became a way of making sense of the Bible that was satisfying intellectually and religiously. The history of the Church's movement from dogmatic to historical approaches in order to make sense and to maintain faith as well as intellectual respectability, has been recapitulated in the lives of countless Christians to the present day.

Dogmatic Interpretation as Horizon of Historical Approach. The historical-critical method in biblical studies operated against the still effective horizon of the dogmatic system. From a contemporary perspective, it is obvious that the earlier dogmatic system dictated the general cognitive and rational nature of meaning sought. It also provided specific dogmatic categories and conclusions, which influenced the application of historical research.[23] The power of the dogmatic approach as the horizon against which the historical-critical method was effective has become apparent in recent years when that dogmatic system (or some dogmatic system) has become lost and attempts have been made to construct a comprehensive theology solely on the basis of historical-critical assumptions and methodologies.

The historical-critical method, then, did not really

serve as the originating basis for meaning. To be satisfying, meanings could not be inconsistent with historical-critical methods and conclusions, but the meaning and significance did not develop simply out of the data uncovered by historical research.

Major Movements in Historical Criticism

In the major movements in historical criticism one may legitimately discern attempts to coordinate historical and religious concerns. The fact that the Bible contains accounts of events in the lives of ancient peoples who actually lived makes the Bible susceptible to historical study at one level. Other levels require attention to the historical context of the writings containing the accounts. Mark, for example, may be studied in the light of its presentation of Jesus' life, or it may be studied in the light of the circumstances that caused it to be written four decades after the time of Jesus. In each of the different levels, meaning was discerned in terms of historical relationships, in terms of the movement from one stage or source of tradition to another, or in terms of the relationship of a unit to a postulated historical situation. The documents were set into frameworks that allowed the discernment of acceptable meaning. The historical approach, then, determined the methodology used and the sorts of meanings discerned.

Source Criticism. An initial concern for historical study focused on the historical events presented in the Bible as the basis for Israel and the Judeo-Christian faith—the Exodus and the Covenant of Sinai in the Old Testament and the life of Jesus in the New

Testament. Historical study's dependence on primary sources led biblical scholars to attempt to sort out the different historical traditions tracing the history of Israel and the life of Jesus. The assumption was that the uncovering of the earliest documents would enable the faithful to read history as it really occurred. It became increasingly clear, however, that the earliest documents were not unbiased reports but rather were theologically impregnated narratives. Nevertheless the historical focus that was responsible for source criticism caused scholars to attempt to analyze the basic documents into earlier written sources and eventually led to research into the oral period prior to the written documents.

Form Criticism. Biblical scholar Hermann Gunkel pioneered the attempt to pry back into the preliterary stages of biblical narrative. He assumed that prior to the written documents of the Old Testament, individual stories had been transmitted, stories that originally existed in an oral form. He also assumed that the earliest documents were basically collections and not original literary creations. Since the stories existed originally as independent units, the study of their formation in the oral period required their study as individual units, and the units could be studied in the light of their functions. A careful study of the unit itself reveals the history of the unit, the results of changes in time and place being reflected in the unit.

Martin Dibelius and Rudolf Bultmann applied the new study of form criticism to the traditional materials contained in Matthew, Mark, and Luke (the synoptic tradition). Dibelius' purpose was to explain by reconstruction and analysis "the origin of the tradition about Jesus, and thus to penetrate into a period previous to that in which our Gospels and their written sources were recorded" and "to make clear the intention and real interest of the earliest tradition."[24] Bultmann wrote with the purpose of "discovering what the original units of the synoptics were, both sayings and stories, to try to establish what this historical setting was, whether they belonged to a primary or secondary tradition or whether they were the product of editorial activity."[25]

Redaction Criticism. Redaction criticism, relying on the insight of the form critical investigation of the earlier history of the tradition, moved its attention to the end of the historical process, the situation and theology of writers and their communities that could be determined by the editorial activity. Willi Marxsen is responsible not only for the name *redaction criticism* but also for the clear distinction between redaction criticism and form criticism. Rudolf Bultmann had traced the history of the synoptic tradition to the composition of the Gospels and declared that this composition "involves nothing in principle new, but only completes what was begun in the oral tradition."[26] Marxsen said that the older form criticism should be called the "form history of the material of synoptic tradition," while the new method of study should be called "form history of the Gospels." The anti-individualistic sociological orientation of the study of the tradition, in the opinion of Marxsen, could not be maintained in the study of the Gospels. The redaction counteracted the fragmentation that took place in the anonymous transmission of material. The counter-reaction of redaction "cannot be explained without taking into account an individual, an author personality who pursues a definite goal with his work."[27]

Interdependence of Meaning and Method

The movement in historical criticism was from source to form to redaction criticism, and we tend to see this movement as a progressive development dependent on the results of earlier research. Certain cause and effect relationships do exist, to be sure. In the beginning, for example, form criticism utilized the results of source analysis. But, in fact, form criticism is not dependent on any one conclusion about documentary relationships. Redaction criticism, again, began as a sort of form criticism of the Gospels as "forms" and was not seen as a separate discipline. Since the evangelists were viewed as editors, the results of source analysis were used. But soon, redaction study was seen as something different from the earlier approach that even called into question the earlier approaches and their conclusions.

The different ways of viewing the biblical material, in fact, developed out of the need to set the material into frameworks that allowed the discernment of sources of meanings that were compatible with different views of historical study. Concern for the knowledge and verification of the events narrated in the Bible (the history of Israel and the life of Jesus) results in viewing the documents as sources for the events described. (Such a concern *can* carry over into form and redaction criticism with attempts to establish the fact that in the oral period the tradition was transmitted accurately and that the redactors were actually cautious and conservative in their editing of the tradition.) Concern for the history of the formation and of the functioning of the literary units at the time of formation results in viewing the units in the light of the historical and sociological situation at the time of formation and not in the light of the history they contain. Contemporary concern for viewing religion as part of a wider network of social relations results in viewing the biblical texts as reflections of social and economic relationships and realities.

What we have observed is a relationship of method to the sort of meaning that is possible and desirable. In both the dogmatic and historical approaches, linguistic and literary tools allow sense to be made of words and sentences. But when the question of meaning goes beyond the paraphrase of the original, differences appear, which grow out of the understanding of the ultimate referent of the text. Augustine's world allowed, or even required, that signs be interpreted in the light of realities beyond the visible world of phenomena, and symbolic interpretation was often required to go beyond plain meaning that had no clear transcendent relationship. But the world transformed by the Enlightenment required that origin and meaning be seen in the light of this world, and the data has been reduced to whatever particular historical idea or ideology is dominant and satisfying.

Existential Interpretation

Meaning and Method in Existential Interpretation

The interdependence of a variety of factors in a total universe of reading and interpretation and the possibility of a nonhistorical focus become visible in the existential approach of Rudolf Bultmann. Again, just as the historical approach operated against the horizon of the dogmatic approach, the existential program must be viewed against the horizon of the prevailing approach, the historical method.

Nature of Meaning Desired. The sort of meaning with which Bultmann is concerned does not grow out of conventional historical conceptualizations and methods. He is interested in a meaning of the New Testament beyond the knowledge of a small area of first-century history. Although he acknowledged the possibility and legitimacy of using the scriptures for historical, and even aesthetic, purposes, Bultmann emphasized that the Bible, as the Word of God, is to be interpreted so that it speaks as Word, for only in this way are faith and new understanding possible. To speak as Word to modern humanity is to speak in terms of human existence. "I think I may take for granted that the right question to frame with regard to the Bible—at any rate within the Church—is the question of human existence." Bultmann gives two reasons for this assumption: the urge that drives him to inquire existentially about his own existence and the proclamation of the Church, which refers him to the scriptures "as the place where I shall hear things about my own existence which vitally concern me."[28] Bultmann may be seen as returning to the "why" question of Augustine. In the light of the scientific and historical revolution and the way that revolution had influenced his own outlook, however, Bultmann is able to question only obliquely about God—in terms of "inquiry into the reality of human existence" which is "inquiry about God and the manifestation of God."[29]

Method Equal to Meaning. As we have seen, there must be a correlation between the question addressed to the text and the method of arriving at an answer. The sort of question (dogmatic, historical) and the method (allegorical, historical-critical) both grow out of a world view that validates the question and the method. In the case of Bultmann's questions, the allegorical method is not acceptable and the historical method could not reach the level desired. The method he found appropriate is that which had been employed in the study of myth, and the categories that could be used to explicate the meanings were those provided by existential philosophy. Doubtless, the availability of method and categories influenced the level of Bultmann's questioning of the text, for the work of Hans Jonas and Martin Heidegger was seminal for Bultmann. In his preface to the first volume of Jonas' *Gnosis und spätantiker Geist* (Gnosticism and the Mind of Late Antiquity), Bultmann declares: "The method of . . . laying hold of the real meaning of a historical phenomenon by means of the principle of analysis of existence, seems to me to have proven brilliantly its fruitfulness. I am certain that this work will fructify research in the history of ideas in many regards, and not least also the interpretation of the New Testament."[30] The work of Martin Heidegger is used for conceptualizing the relevant concepts for speaking of human existence. Bultmann denies that in his utilization of Heidegger he is suggesting a "final philosophical system" or that exegesis is supposed to "take over the actual answer that philosophy gives to the existential questions of the meaning of my own particular existence."[31] For Bultmann, the act that makes the move to faith possible is the decisive act of God in the cross of Christ. This makes possible the authentic life of humanity and is not to be demythologized. Hence, theology and existential philosophy could not be equated. Nevertheless in scientific study of the Bible, the questions asked must be those that may be answered by scientific method.

Horizon of Historical Criticism

Historical conceptualizations and methods constituted the horizon against which existential interpretation developed and actually formed an important ingredient in the method. Historical criticism was not seen by Bultmann as being in opposition with his purpose but as insufficient for his purpose. Nevertheless Bultmann maintained his historical research while carrying out his theological synthesis, and there was transaction between the two. The theological synthesis could not be inconsistent with the possibility of historical reconstruction, nor could historical reconstruction be inconsistent with the theological synthesis. The interdependence of theological synthesis and historical reconstruction is seen in Bultmann's reaction to the question of the quest for the historical Jesus.

Bultmann had concluded that a quest for the historical Jesus, as carried out in the nineteenth century, was impossible because of the nature of the sources. But just as important for Bultmann was the conclusion that the quest for the historical Jesus was unnecessary and illegitimate, since the object of Christian faith is not the historical Jesus. The real Christ event is the proclamation of the Church. This proclamation cannot be used as a source for reconstructing the historic Jesus. The Lord is not the historic Jesus, but Jesus Christ as encountered in the proclamation.

Beginning in the early 1950s, students of Bultmann began to question the illegitimacy and impossibility of the quest for the historical Jesus. They concluded that the theological necessity of a new quest grew out of the proclamation of the Church itself. The gospel is not just the story of the earthly Jesus, but neither is it just the proclamation of a mythological, preexistent, and exalted Lord. James M. Robinson declared, "It is this concern of the *kerygma* for the historicity of Jesus which necessitates a new quest."[32] The altered perception of the legitimacy of the quest caused even the students of Bultmann to take a different attitude toward the possibility of such a quest and the sources that provided a means for the quest as well as for proclamation. On July 25, 1959, Bultmann responded to the new questers. His conceptualization of the kerygma caused him to continue to deny the possibility and legitimacy of the quest. He admitted that the kerygma presupposes the historical Jesus and that without the historical Jesus there would be no kerygma. But the kerygma only presupposes the fact that Jesus was; the kerygma is not interested in the content and character of Jesus' history. The use of historical research to legitimize the kerygma is the denial of the nature of the kerygma.[33]

The Contemporary Challenge of Interpretation

Analysis of the various approaches to the Bible uncovers the same basic procedure: Readers make sense of the Bible in the light of their world, which includes not only linguistic and literary tools but also world views that influence the sorts of meanings and the methods that are satisfying. World view and corresponding method influence the perception and use of the linguistic and literary data and *vice versa*. Neither the dogmatic nor the existential approach makes sense as a method for uncovering historical facts and relationships. The historical approach, on the other hand, makes no sense as a method for bringing to light the ahistorical or trans-historical values that lie behind or beyond historical phenomena. We are beginning to see that reading and interpretation involved a universe of interdependent systems.

The challenge today is that the factors involved in interpretation are dynamic. They will not stand still! The views of self, world, text, language, and meaning continue to change. How can interpretation take place within a dynamically expanding system, consisting of dynamic elements?

We may attempt to refute or ignore the implications of the sort of interdependence or relativism involved. The particular universe within which we make sense is so compelling that it is difficult to appreciate the relativism of methods and meanings. We "know" intuitively and emotionally that the meanings validated by our experience in our world are true in some final way. Even when we recognize intellectually the inevitability of some type of relativism, we attempt to ignore or refute it because relativism seems to mean that all of our facts are false or at least that no important fact can be verified.

It is possible to reevaluate the relationship among universe, meaning, and method as indicating not that truth is unattainable but that it is attainable in all the various universes. Truth is discovered and expressed in terms that make sense within a particular universe of meaning. It is not some final objective trans-historical and trans-human expression of truth, for truth in such a form does not touch us. But meanings that are consistent with the various systems that cohere in a particular universe of meaning are true—or truthful. The universe, of course, includes us, the inhabitants of that universe who use such truth in making sense for ourselves—sense of our universe and of ourselves—but it also includes elements over against us, which are involved in our making sense of the world and of ourselves.

For the student who has been immersed in historical principles and methods, this idea of meaning and truth—or truthfulness—may sound strange. It may, however, be seen as an extrapolation from the basic principles of historical criticism—the principles of the relatedness and interdependence of the phenomena of human historical life and of finding meaning of cultural phenomena in the light of one's own experience.

Instead of giving up any attempt to find meaning, we may observe that human beings continue to make sense and to build upon that common sense observation. Even if the sense is not some final synthesis of meaning, a meaning is discovered or created, which is satisfying for the present location of the reader. This meaning is a result of the nexus of signifying systems, which include the reader or the readership. Since these systems are dynamic, meaning is dynamic, and *final meaning* continues to recede.

Early Russian and Czech formalists and structuralists emphasized the dynamic relationship between textual form and content and historically constrained, and yet constantly changing, conventions and codes. The difference today is that we are conscious of the relational and dynamic nature of literature and its meaning and significance at the very time we are reading and criticizing the text. For the formalists and structuralists, the relationship was historical; for us, the relationship is not only historical but also personal. Today, we may choose the schema or the framework with which and within which we seek meaning. We may recapitulate in ourselves (individually and as a group) those changes that the early structuralists saw in terms of historical evolution.

Such awareness should not disable us, but it should make us humble. In our interpretative activities, we take up our location, and we make sense of the text. Indirectly and obliquely we make sense of ourselves and of our world. The reader's involvement does not mean that "anything goes." There is a validation of meaning and significance, but this validation—just as the determination of meaning and significance—takes into account the total nexus of dynamic signifying systems. There have been other senses, and these were not illusions. There will be other senses; indeed, there *are* other senses. This does not disable us; it enables us to make sense in the light of our world and of our own psychological and sociological sets and situations. The reader becomes the touchstone or schema.

This vision of pluralism may be a nightmare. It may be that we are, in the words of Dan Via, simply between the Bultmanns[34]—that is, perhaps one world view will overwhelm us and a new "Bultmann," who has internalized that world view, will capture our allegiance and bring a type of unity that does not now exist. I think not. Our community of biblical scholars will, in my opinion, cooperate in the future not by a commitment to a monolithic method validated by one compelling world view. Our cooperation will come by recognizing the inevitability and richness of diversity. We will not recapitulate the particular dogmatic method of Augustine, but we will recognize what was happening in that method once thought of as so illogical. We may appreciate the fact that the same thing is happening with us and gain guidance from a new look at the interdependence of factors that continue to operate in our reading and interpretation.

Notes

1. Rudolf Bultmann, "The Problem of Hermeneutics," in *Essays Philosophical and Theological,* trans. James C. Greig (London: SCM, 1955), pp. 257, 259.

2. The "proper" approach to the Bible has been self-evidently the one dictated by some academic or religious authority. This way of determining the correct approach is not only the easiest, but it is also in keeping with the sociology of knowledge, for, as Peter Berger says, "Most of what we 'know' we have taken on the authority of others, and it is only as others continue to confirm this 'knowledge' that it continues to be plausible to us. It is such socially shared, socially taken-for-granted 'knowledge' that allows us to move with a measure of confidence through everyday life." *A Rumor of Angels: Modern Society and the Rediscovery of the Supernatural,* (Garden City, N.Y.: Anchor Books, 1970), p. 6.

3. Augustine, *On the Catechising of the Uninstructed,* in volume 3 of A Select Library of the Nicene and Post-Nicene Fathers of the Christian Church series, ed. Philip Schaff (Grand Rapids, Mich.: Wm. B. Eerdman's Co., 1956), 19.32.

4. Cited in C. H. Dodd, *The Parables of the Kingdom* (New York: Charles Scribner's Sons, 1961), p. 1. For many contemporary scholars, allegory and Augustine's method were demolished by the mere citation of Augustine's interpretation of that parable in C. H. Dodd's influential book.

5. Augustine, *On the Profit of Believing,* 14.31. Cited in Gerald Bonner, "Augustine as Biblical Scholar," in *Cambridge History of the Bible,* vol. 1, "From the Beginnings to Jerome," eds. P. R. Ackroyd and C. F. Evans (Cambridge, England: Cambridge University Press, 1970), p. 553.

6. Gerald Bonner, *St. Augustine of Hippo: Life and*

Controversies (Philadelphia: The Westminster Press, 1963), p. 229.

7. Bonner, "Augustine as Biblical Scholar," p. 561.

8. Augustine, *On Christian Doctrine*, in volume 2 of A Select Library of the Nicene and Post-Nicene Fathers of the Christian Church series, ed. Philip Schaff (Grand Rapids, Mich.: Wm. B. Eerdman's Co., 1956), pref., sec. 9.

9. Augustine, *Letters*, 120.3.13. In Bonner, *St. Augustine of Hippo: Life and Controversies*, p. 224.

10. Bonner, *St. Augustine of Hippo*, pp. 133-34.

11. Peter Brown, *Augustine of Hippo* (Berkeley: University of California Press, 1967), p. 98.

12. Northrop Frye, *The Great Code: The Bible and Literature* (New York: Harcourt Brace Jovanovich, 1982), pp. 7-8. Frye follows Giambattista in distinguishing three stages of language.

13. Jurij Lotman, *The Structure of the Artistic Text*, Michigan Slavic Contributions 7, trans. Gail Lenhoff and Ronald Vroon (Ann Arbor: University of Michigan Press, 1977), p. 125. The system of Augustine necessarily involving indirect access through signs may be conceivable today by noting the similarity between that system and the way a therapist makes contact with the inner world of a child through patterns emerging in the child's artistic creation or through play with sand, water, and brick. See Brown, *Augustine of Hippo*, p. 252.

14. Brown, *Augustine of Hippo*, p. 253.

15. Ibid.

16. Lotman, *The Structure of the Artistic Text*, p. 267.

17. Bonner, "Augustine as Biblical Scholar," p. 554.

18. Frye, *The Great Code*, p. 13.

19. Descartes' *Regulae ad directionem ingenii* (Rules for the Direction of the Mind) was written in the 1620s and published in 1701. His *Discourse on Method* was published in 1637. Leszek Kolakowski says that "modern European philosophy . . . consists of footnotes to Descartes" ("Descartes, Rene," in *The Encyclopedia of Religion*, vol. 4 (New York: Macmillan, 1987), p. 298).

20. Ernst Troeltsch, "Historiography," in *Encyclopedia of Religion and Ethics*, vol. 4, ed. James Hastings (New York: Charles Scribner's Sons, 1925), p. 718. See also his essay on "Contingency."

21. In his essay "Über historische und dogmatische Methode in der Theologie" (On Historical and Dogmatic Method in Theology), *Gesammelte Schriften*, vol. 2 (Tübingen, J.C.B. Mohr, 1913), pp. 729-53, Troeltsch applied the principles of correlation, criticism, and analogy to challenge the dogmatic understanding of Jesus as the exclusive revelation of God and the traditional isolation of Christianity from other religions.

22. Van A. Harvey, *The Historian and the Believer: The Morality of Historical Knowledge and Christian Belief* (New York: Macmillan, 1966), p. 6.

23. Helmut Koester has acknowledged and lamented the fact that historical critical activity as exemplified in the genre of New Testament "introduction"

> in spite of its great erudition has never managed to become an enterprise which is central for the vital interests of religious, theological and historical understanding. At best, it has been useful as an ancillary discipline, helping to secure genuine source-materials for scholars who wanted to base their discussions on reliable information; or aiding theologians who wanted to affirm the authenticity of canonical writings on which they based their doctrines and dogmas. (Helmut Koester, "New Testament Introduction: A Critique of a Discipline," in *Christianity, Judaism and Other Greco-Roman Cults: Studies for Morton Smith at Sixty*, part one [Leiden: E. J. Brill, 1975], p. 6.)

24. Martin Dibelius, *From Tradition to Gospel*, trans. Bertram Lee Woolf (New York: Charles Scribner's Sons, 1935), p. iii.

25. Rudolf Bultmann, *The History of the Synoptic Tradition*, trans. John Marsh (New York: Harper, 1963), pp. 2-3.

26. Ibid., p. 321.

27. Willi Marxsen, *Mark the Evangelist: Studies on the Redaction History of the Gospel*, trans. James Boyce et al. (Nashville: Abingdon Press, 1969), p. 18.

28. Rudolf Bultmann, "Bultmann Replies to His Critics," in *Kerygma and Myth*, vol. 1, ed. Hans Werner Bartsch (New York: Harper Torchbooks, 1961), pp. 191-92.

29. Bultmann, "The Problem of Hermeneutics," p. 258.

30. Hans Jonas, *Gnosis und spätantiker Geist*, vol. 1 (Göttingen: Vandenhoeck & Ruprecht, 1934), p. xvii.

31. Bultmann, "Bultmann Replies to His Critics," p. 193.

32. James M. Robinson, *A New Quest of the Historical Jesus* (London: SCM, 1959), p. 88.

33. Rudolf Bultmann, "The Primitive Christian Kerygma and the Historical Jesus," in *The Historical Jesus and the Kerygmatic Christ*, eds. and trans. Carl E. Braaten and Roy A. Harrisville (Nashville: Abingdon Press, 1964), p. 42.

34. Dan O. Via, Jr., "A Quandary of Contemporary New Testament Scholarship: The Time Between the 'Bultmanns,' " *Journal of Religion* 55 (1975):456-61.

Chapter Two

Toward the Postmodern:

Historical-Hermeneutic Approaches

The desire to find and exploit fresh meaning of biblical texts is evident in attempts to complement, modify, and move beyond the once-satisfying historical paradigm.[1] This chapter is designed to examine approaches to interpreting biblical texts that are not essentially or solely historically oriented but that remain in dialogue with the historical-critical tradition. The horizons of previous dogmatic and historical approaches, however, provide control and constitute limitations for the new approaches.

A general limitation of previous approaches is the view of the biblical text as the result of a cause, the exteriorization of some dogmatic or historical, sociological or psychological, reality. The function of the reader in this conceptualization is to devise an objective method capable of establishing the cause and to give the meaning (the cause) in appropriate concepts. The consciousness of the reader's transactive relationship with the text (the text being conceptualized in the light of the reader's needs and capacity and the reader's needs and capacity being affected by the text) is eclipsed because of the demand to treat the text as an object of the reader's critical scrutiny.

This chapter will demonstrate the need to move beyond present conceptualizations of the nature of biblical studies and the role and function of the biblical text to a concept that will consciously make the reader a focus of concern. It will show that meaning is in part a result of the creative involvement of the reader and that present conceptualizations unnecessarily limit or obscure the possibility and reality of the reader's use of imagination in interpretation.

Historical Meaning and History-like Application

A popular strategy is to supplement the historical approach by applying the results to the interpreter's contemporary situation. It is assumed that an original historical meaning may be uncovered by historical-critical method independent of the significance of the present and that the sorts of meaning discerned by historical method may be related in a satisfying way to present-day significance.

The power of the evolutionary-historical model caused it to be the model not only for discovering original meaning but also for finding a significance or for making application. History-like models of application were satisfying for the same reason that the historical method was satisfying: They were consistent with the contemporary world view. The historical mode of application was particularly powerful in an early period of emphasis on "progressive revelation" and in a more recent period of biblical theology's emphasis on the action of God in history. The religious or theological message of the past and present was perceived in terms of origins and development. Although factors beyond history and criticism were involved (and we may classify these methods as history-like instead of as history), advocates of these approaches saw them as being grounded not in dogmatic assertions or speculation but in empirical inquiry, capable of scientific verification.

Progressive Revelation

Progressive revelation was a method of application satisfying to nineteenth century scholarship. The original meaning was to be ascertained "with the aid of every scientific skill at our disposal," then the significance of the passage in the "development of the biblical revelation as a whole" was to be perceived. "Only then shall we be in a position to comprehend its meaning for us in the changed situation of today."[2] By the close of the nineteenth century, biblical study was accommodated to historical study through the idea that God revealed truth as people were able to understand it.

> The conceptualization of "progressive revelation" enabled the enlightened and sensitive modern conscience to understand why it was necessary that the Bible should record the partial gropings and even the positive misconceptions of earlier ages; the Bible is the record of the religious education of the human race. . . . Every partial insight of Israel's long religious development was gathered, when at last men were prepared and able to receive it, into the final revelation of his truth which God gave to the world in Jesus Christ.[3]

This method of correlation was fully in accord with the spirit of the age, the spirit of optimism and belief in people's capacity to realize their splendid potentiality in the future. Progressive revelation as the key to the understanding of the Bible was just as natural as the belief that progress was the key to the understanding of history and society. The historical method used in the framework of progressive revelation accomplished for the nineteenth and early twentieth centuries what the allegorical method accomplished for the ancient and medieval church: the reconciliation of scriptural teaching with changing views of the universe and the rationalization of ethical injunctions and practices that could no longer commend themselves to the enlightened conscience.[4]

Biblical Theology

The approach of *biblical theology* in America in the mid-twentieth century is parallel to the approach of progressive revelation. In the case of biblical theology, however, the emphasis is not on progressive revelation of truth consistent with the human capacity to comprehend such truth.[5] In biblical theology, the emphasis is on the action of God in history. Just as in the case of progressive revelation, however, the acts-of-God framework for the exercise of biblical criticism is seen as a result of critical empirical inquiry. The theology of the acts of God provided both the framework for critical investigation and the basis for satisfying contemporary signification.

Krister Stendahl's article "Contemporary Biblical

Theology" illustrates the approach of biblical theology at its best. Stendahl sees a genuine division between past meaning and present significance. But the division is not total because twentieth-century historical research has made visible a past meaning completely compatible with present significance.[6] "The bridge between the centuries of biblical events and our own time" is found in the "actual history of the church as still ongoing sacred history of God's people." The basis Stendahl offers for the normative function of scripture is "the act of faith by which Israel and its sister by adoption, the church, recognizes its history as sacred history, and finds in these writings the epitome of the acts of God." Stendahl supposes that it is in preaching "where the meaning of the original meets with the meaning for today" and the key for the preacher is the conception of "the Christian existence as a life by the fruits of God's acts in Jesus Christ." In treating the resurrection texts, for example, the preacher would "place the emphasis where the texts themselves put it and . . . meditate . . . along the lines of how the power of the new age manifested itself in Jesus Christ, not only as a token of our resurrection, but as the enthronement of Christ and as the possibility for man to live by the powers of the new age here and now."[7]

Stendahl's approach concludes with the need and capacity of modern men and women, which goes beyond the sort of meaning that can be uncovered by historical methods *per se.* In a creative fashion, the biblical data are conceptualized to make room for the meaning with which Stendahl is concerned. But since the claim of objectivity is made, criticism cannot ignore biblical theology's attempt to justify the framework for meaning on the basis of conventional descriptive historical method. Ironically, the final blow to biblical theology was delivered by James Barr the very year that Stendahl's article was published. Barr's basic criticism is that biblical theology does not take seriously the biblical text itself. Biblical theology is not developed from, and only from, *all* of the Bible. An abstraction that emphasizes sacred history works only on a small portion of the Bible.[8]

Values and Limitations of History-like Application

The value of evolutionary-historical approaches must not be underestimated. The basic value is that the approaches are "within the truth" of a discourse used effectively in the nineteenth and twentieth centuries to make sense of cultural phenomena. The procedure of reducing the text to an object that can be subjected to historical method allows results that can be verified by others on the basis of the same method. This method has allowed scholars from all religious and from no religious persuasions to cooperate in biblical scholarship. Questions aimed at the text can be answered to the satisfaction of critics on the basis of more comprehensive scientific historical postulates. Theological models using the evolutionary-historical model in a heuristic way are valuable to the degree that the evolutionary-historical model is satisfying and, therefore, to the degree that a sizable number of scholars agree on the validity of a particular history-like theological framework for making sense of biblical texts.

The limitations of historical and history-like methods have become obvious. A major limitation is the identification of theological method with a culturally and temporally limited historical ideology. The demand that the meta-historical framework for understanding the biblical data be derived from only the data has limited the sorts of questions addressed to the text and the meanings found in the biblical text. Meta-historical questions that can be correlated to theological systems become suspect because they are not susceptible to historical evidence and proof alone. "What" questions are asked because they can be answered. The methodological limitations may then be taken not simply as methodological but as epistemological. The historical level of research alone may be seen as "within the truth" of scholarly discourse and may cause scholars to turn their backs on "application" as illegitimate and nonrespectable.

Other sorts of limitations become obvious when readers and critics are determined that original historical meaning is not sufficient and that present-day significance or application must follow the determination of original meaning. The rigorous, scientific demands on historical-critical study result in conclusions that are either too tenuous to use for satisfying theological and religious application or that are too limited for complete and comprehensive application. The attempt to rediscover the teachings of Jesus, for example, may be motivated by the desire to find material for religious teaching and proclamation. The critical historian is not willing to attribute to Jesus all the sayings put on his lips by the writers of the Gospels. The application of tests of authenticity that are critically satisfying, however, may end up with a core of sayings that are not theologically and religiously satisfying—and that admittedly do not reflect the full range of what Jesus actually taught.

The model of biblical interpretation that sees application built upon the "assured results" of historical-critical research, then, will result in a truncated application, in a forsaking of application, or in an application that is not really dependent on critical study. Students may find themselves mastering sophisticated historical-critical tools in academic biblical study, but may find a quite different and often uncritical force at work in preaching or even in academic theological studies.

The present work advocates the continuation of the historical-critical method, but not with the view that adequate formulation of meaning-for-the-reader can be achieved on the basis of the results of such a method *per se*. The historical-critical method and its results will form a system that must be coordinated with other systems. A historical scholar may give more attention to the historical question, but will not confuse the answers to the "what" questions with answers to the "why" questions. What sort of coordination is desirable? How may it be achieved? Is it possible to remain critical in an approach that relativizes the historical-critical method and its results?

The Redefinition of Historical Method

Scholars cannot objectively reconstruct the events recounted in the Bible or those surrounding the origins of the biblical writings themselves. Source critics have been unable to peel off layers of tradition to obtain a contemporaneous and objective account of what happened. (Even accounts contemporaneous with the events would not be unaffected by the perceptions of the observers, of course.) Form criticism became the acceptable method between the First and Second World Wars in part because of source criticism's inability to uncover sources contemporaneous with the events described. In the redaction criticism developing after the Second World War, the historical moment of concern was that of Israel's theologians and the Christian evangelists and their churches. In all of these historical approaches, the limitations of historical criticism has become evident.

Redefinition of the Historical Moment: Canonical Criticism

Canonical criticism may be understood as the move to the historical period subsequent to those with which source, form, and redaction criticism are concerned. Brevard Childs and James A. Sanders are the pioneers in canonical criticism, with Childs being concerned with the analysis of the final form of the biblical books and Sanders concerned with the hermeneutical principles used in the process of canonization. Although these two scholars differ in their approaches, they illustrate not only the dissatisfaction with conventional form and redaction criticism, but also the need to move beyond any form of a conventional historical paradigm.

Brevard Childs is less concerned with discovering

the hermeneutical principles used in the process of canonization than in analyzing the final form of the biblical books.

> Canonical analysis focuses its attention on the final form of the text itself. It seeks neither to use the text merely as a source for other information obtained by means of an oblique reading, nor to reconstruct a history of religious development. Rather, it treats the literature in its own integrity. Its concern is not to establish a history of Hebrew literature in general, but to study the features of this peculiar set of religious texts in relation to their usage within the historical community of ancient Israel. To take the canonical shape of these texts seriously is to seek to do justice to a literature which Israel transmitted as a record of God's revelation to his people along with Israel's response.[9]

Childs denies that this approach stifles genuine exegetical activity by bringing dogmatic categories to bear. "Rather, the approach seeks to work within that interpretive structure which the biblical text has received from those who formed and used it as sacred scripture. To understand that canonical shape requires the highest degree of exegetical skill in an intensive wrestling with the text."[10]

Sanders used the term *canonical criticism* in his book *Torah and Canon* to indicate a method of study that "picks up with the results of tradition criticism and goes on to ask what the *function* or *authority* was of the ancient tradition in the context where cited. How was it used? Canonical criticism takes the measure of the authority that the ancient tradition exercised in the context of its use."[11]

Canonical criticism for Sanders, then, is more than a study of the final shaping of the Bible.

Nevertheless it is the product of an evolution from an early interest in the sources that went into the literary makeup of the Bible through a concern with smaller units and sources to the larger literary units in the final stages of composition. In that process, Sanders says, "One can actually see how the next step . . . would evolve into interest as to how the large literary units (whole biblical books or large sections of Scripture) finally came together into the several canons which we inherit from antiquity."[12]

Sanders is most concerned with the hermeneutic prolongation of the biblical text, the spanning of the gap between modern cultural systems of meaning and original meanings, which may be recovered through critical method. The task of spanning the gap may be called *canonical hermeneutics.* It is "the means whereby Israel, Judaism, and the church spanned the gaps between inherited faith and new cultural settings."[13] Sanders sees the process of spanning the gaps, as well as the emerging traditions of the process, as canonical. "The canon includes the process whereby early authoritative traditions encountered ancient cultural challenges, were rendered adaptable to those challenges, and thus themselves were formed and re-formed according to the needs of the believing communities."[14] The canonical approach is a result of the insight that the Bible is a product of history. "But it is a product of a very peculiar history . . . a history which continues today in Jewish and Christian believing communities." Canonical criticism, then, is "a confession on the part of biblical criticism that it now recognizes that the true *Sitz-im-Leben* today of the Bible is in the believing communities—heirs to the first shapers of this literature—whatever the provenance . . . of the original forms and early literary units."[15]

Is it possible that the historical mooring of the hermeneutical enterprise in canonical criticism is a limitation that must be transcended? In hermeneutics, moves that are not essentially historical in nature are necessary. In the movement beyond conventional historical interests to hermeneutical concerns, canonical critics would seem to benefit from contemporary hermeneutical insights and concern for meaning "in front of the text." But Childs declares that philosophical hermeneutics in the tradition of Paul Ricoeur is as incompatible with the canonical approach as are various forms of historicism. Such a hermeneutical approach

> fails to take seriously the essential function of the canon in grounding the biblical metaphors within the context of historic Israel. By shaping Israel's traditions into the form of a normative scripture the biblical idiom no longer functions for the community of faith as free-floating metaphor, but as the divine imperative and promise to a historically conditioned people of God whose legacy the Christian church confesses to share.[16]

Childs is not unsympathetic to the hermeneutical enterprise, of course. He sees that "it is constitutive of the canon to seek to transmit the tradition in such a way as to prevent its being moored in the past. Actualization derives from a hermeneutical concern which was present during the different stages of the book's canonization. It is built into the structure of the text itself, and reveals an enormous richness of theological interpretation by which to render the text religiously accessible."[17] Childs credits the modern hermeneutical impasse, however, to the disregard for canonical shaping. "The usual critical method of biblical exegesis is, first, to seek to restore an original historical setting by stripping away those very elements which constitute the canonical shape. Little wonder that once the biblical text has been securely anchored in the historical past by 'decanonizing' it, the interpreter has difficulty applying it to the modern religious context."[18]

Is the canonical approach not another way of anchoring the biblical text in the historical past? In spite of the initial liberation of canonical criticism (against the horizon of earlier concentration on pre-canonical forms), is that criticism in a radical form not simply another way of stripping away the possibility of applying the text in the modern religious context—at least for those who are no longer persuaded by the assumptions that have sustained the historical paradigm?

Revised Historical Method: Stuhlmacher's New Biblical Theology

The move from source to form and redaction criticism directed attention away from the events described in the biblical texts and created skepticism about their historicity. Rudolf Bultmann stated a skeptical criterion, which became widely accepted as the only way to establish authentic Jesus tradition in the light of form critical assumptions: "We can only count on possessing a genuine similitude of Jesus, where, on the one hand, expression is given to the contrast between Jewish morality and piety and the distinctive eschatological temper which characterized the preaching of Jesus; and where on the other hand we find no specific Christian features."[19]

The factual character of events described in the biblical texts has led to a contemporary biblical theology that relies not on a methodologically skeptical historical criticism but on a redefined historical method. The most comprehensive attempt to revise postulates and procedures in historical criticism is the new biblical theology movement associated with the work of Peter Stuhlmacher, a student of Ernst Käsemann and professor at the University of Tübingen. In order to appreciate the problematic of the historical mode as such, the work of Stuhlmacher will be observed in the stages represented by the two editions of his major work on hermeneutics, *Vom Verstehen des Neuen Testaments: Eine Hermeneutik.*[20] His work as a whole is to be seen not simply as a chipping away at some of the "assured results" of New Testament research in the Bultmannian tradition but as an overhauling of the basic framework. The skeptical procedures of historical criticism are challenged and replaced by a hermeneutics of consent (*Einverständnis,* "common understanding," "mutual understanding," or "empathy") paralleling Adolf Schlatter's hermeneutics of "observation" (*Wahrnehmung*).

Schlatter as Model. In the early decades of this century, Schlatter protested the methodologically skeptical historical method (termed the "atheistic method"). According to Schlatter, criticism is required because a revelation that discloses God apart from and separate from human beings does not exist. The glory of God is not that God is capable of being the author of an inerrant book but that God has entered into a relationship with mortals so that as mortals they could speak God's word.[21] Criticism, however, is not simply exercised by an autonomous subject examining history as an object. It is exercised by observing the historical events that lie behind the traditional texts, events in which the certainty of God for individuals and for humankind as a whole is produced.[22] The theologian has the duty not only of observing the religious event but of grasping the event with a resolute devotion to the theologian's own purposes and perspectives. The method of the historical exegete must be appropriate to both the biblical text and the exegete's object:[23]

> Observation is no empty word; that wonderful capacity to see is granted to us, even in the historical field, even for processes which form the inner life of man and of mankind . . . It is we who must see and our eyes are the structures of thought which we carry in ourselves. Therefore, it is not a matter of indifference as to which "leitmotifs" are used by us in observation. If we wish to explain religion from the perspective of the world, from the beginning onward we set ourselves in a radical opposition to our object which will not be explained from the perspective of the world but which asserts the idea of God loudly and persistently. Our object desires that we think of God; the observer wishes to think "without including the idea of God." The sharp conflict of wills is present; can we still perceive in spite of this? The more we desire not only to observe but also to explain and the more the object will be included in our complete schema, the stronger becomes the scientific caricature and the more certain the alleged science is

transformed in polemic against its object with the work of fiction arising which does not testify to the series of events but to the historian.[24]

Stuhlmacher's Reconstituted Historical Method. Stuhlmacher recapitulates the arguments of Schlatter against the background of the work of Bultmann and his students. In both editions of his *Hermeneutik,* Stuhlmacher insists upon the historical nature of the biblical writings and the historical nature of the events to which they witness. "The Bible is a book of history. Each of its books was written in a definite historical situation by men for men. Therefore, the Bible is treated most legitimately when the exposition takes account of the historical character of scripture and makes perceivable in it the witness of God which transcends all times."[25] In the first edition, Stuhlmacher gives attention to the modification of the historical method, with the assumption that a modified historical method will match the function of the Bible. The biblical texts witness to a reality that the principles of historical study, as enunciated by Troeltsch, are not capable of perceiving: a witness of God that transcends particular historical periods; a witness of truth that is constitutive for human life, the truth incarnate in Jesus Christ; a witness of the work of Jesus as Messianic reconciler (*VVNT,* 1st ed., pp. 207, 219, 220, 223). The purpose of the Bible, which is seen clearly by historical observation, is to engender faith.[26]

If historical method is necessary, and the method is to deal with life-giving and life-sustaining forces, with the witness of God made perceivable in the historical linguistic documents, then historical method must be more than or different from the conventional historical method. It must be an instrument that has the capacity of dealing with the purpose of confrontation with the biblical texts and their world (*VVNT*, p. 219). Stuhlmacher suggested that the principle of perception must be used alongside the principles delineated by Troeltsch. Through the power of this principle, we may regain the possibility of discovering in history something new and without analogy. A new search may be inaugurated for the powers in the tradition that may establish and sustain life.

Stuhlmacher not only attempted to reformulate historical method to allow the study he envisions, but he also applied the principles and sketched a biblical theology of Jesus as the messianic reconciler. Jesus "was the messianic son of man and reconciler whose word and work aim at bringing God and the men of his time into peace with God and thereby into salvation." This theology is "the historical substance of the Gospel . . . the quintessence of the work of Jesus."[27]

In the second edition of his *Hermeneutik,* Stuhmacher does not allow the historical-critical approach (even a modified historical criticism) to carry the full weight of biblical study. Rather, he situates historical criticism within a more comprehensive model. In the second edition, Stuhlmacher also omits the historical reconstruction accomplished by the revised historical method. He concludes, rather, with a reformulated model of biblical interpretation, about which he declares: "The ecclesiastical interpretation of Scripture proposed by us is not exhausted with the description of the text as a historical phenomenon. It begins with and serves the present (ecclesiastical) use of Scripture" (*VVNT*, 2nd ed., p. 242).

Stuhlmacher distinguishes two major processes in his later work. An initial process of analysis involves the attempt to illuminate the texts themselves and the process behind their creation in their historical individuality. The second phase grows out of this initial move; it is the actual process of interpretation, which is accomplished in three steps. In the first step, the text is traced again as precisely as possible in its original setting and with all aspects of its "world" taken into consideration. The second step involves the placing of the particular text with its affirmation in the total canonical context of the Old and New Testaments and the evaluation of the text in this framework. The final step is the development of an interpretation that speaks directly to the present. Such an interpretation

> is undertaken in light of the history of the interpretation and influence of the text and of the mature dogma resulting from the ecclesiastical interpretation of Scripture. In the process of the work historical and dogmatic considerations and evaluations are interlaced. . . . Through the conscious interlacing of historical analysis and dogmatically-reflective interpretation we avoid an historical-critical biblicism which deludes itself into believing that it is exempt from all dogmatic responsibilities, and also avoids the different varieties of a pure dogmatic use of Scripture which is no longer historically responsible. (*VVNT*, 2nd ed., pp. 241-42)

Stuhlmacher's insight that the historical mode of criticism alone is not able to exhaust the potentiality of meaning is an abiding value of his studies. The meaning and significance of the text are not limited to those meanings that conventional historical criticism is designed to recover. Meaning is not reduced to the nexus of historical relationships. Text is not simply a historical source. There is no contradiction between historical study and the more comprehensive model, for the text is *intended* to produce an effect on the reader, in part perhaps by the quasi-literary activity of the reader's imaginative reconstruction of events that explain the formation of the text.

In a comprehensive model, less attention is given to the textual elements as traditions to be traced in historical evolution, and more attention is given to the formation of the textual elements in the structures of a completed literary work. A *critical* method is envisioned, which sees meaning in terms of a nexus that includes not only the structures of the completed literary work but also the reader and those sorts of values and meanings that impinge upon the reader.

Evaluation of Method. The value of the work of Professor Stuhlmacher is indisputable. Regardless of the criticism of the way he chose to elaborate his method and of the historical conceptualization he arrived at by use of this method in the first edition, Stuhlmacher was dealing with serious questions in a serious way. The conventional historical approaches as such were no longer satisfying because the questioning and answering of the text within such approaches did not exhaust the potential of the text for meaning. Stuhlmacher's efforts to contain present-day application of the Bible within the historical-critical paradigm is evidence of the power of that world view and mind-set. Students were enabled imaginatively to construct from the text historical traditions and events behind texts that relate to a trans-historical witness and to the interests and lives of the students. One reason for the effectiveness of the approach (as was true of the biblical theology movement in America) is its kinship to a critical approach to cultural phenomena that has been satisfying and productive for over a century. It sees the text as a result of causes that are manifested in human experiences. By an analysis of the textual tradition, these causes may be discerned.

The limitations of Stuhlmacher's modified historical approach were the mirror-images of the values—that is, the history-like approach was mistaken for an attempt to do history in the older mode and was, therefore, found wanting. The scrupulous application of criteria for authenticity in the new quest for the historical Jesus, for example, was not duplicated in Stuhlmacher's work because of his fundamental disagreement with the foundations of the methodologically skeptical historical method and its inability to do justice to the nature of the text. For those trained in the rigorous application of historical criticism, the modified historical approach was not satisfying. The history-like mode promised results verifiable by conventional criticism; such was not forthcoming. The reformulation of the historical method was in effect a repudiation of the method as accepted and practiced by New

Testament historians. Stuhlmacher, in fact, saw that the introduction of his principle of perception stood in opposition to the classical principles of historical criticism (*VVNT*, 1st ed., p. 220).

The adherence to a history-like method formally equivalent to rigorous (or skeptical) historical procedures must be seen as finally more of a limitation than a value. It constrains unnecessarily the perceptions of the reader and the meaning and function of the text. If meaning is not to be limited to the sort of meaning that can be gathered from the historical nexus, why be limited to a method designed to ascertain such meaning?

The value of Stuhlmacher's work (which is still in progress) is the movement from a history-like (a quasi-literary) method, which is still operating with the constraints of historical method, to a more liberated and liberating method, which is able to remain faithful to the text and to the reader's needs and capacities. Stuhlmacher acknowledges that in interpretation we are moved by a "pre-understanding," a "perception-directing interest," which gives the direction of our interpretation. His role as a theologian of the church and his context in the Protestant Theological faculty of the University of Tübingen influence his interest and perception. Stuhlmacher himself, therefore, is concerned to explicate a method that is appropriate for the needs and uses of the church, but his model moves beyond a history-like process.

Revised Historical Method: Sociological Interpretation

Sociological interpretation may be seen as a continuation of the historical-critical, but with different reference points. For historical criticism, the textual reference points were political and religious. For sociological interpretation, what is central are social referents, explicit or implied. Norman Gottwald describes the method.

> Sociological exegesis tries to situate a biblical book or subsection in its proper social setting—taking into account the literary and historical relations between the parts and the whole. It further attempts to illuminate the text according to its explicit or implied social referents, in a manner similar to historical-critical method's clarification of the political and religious reference points of text.[28]

In *The Hebrew Bible: A Socio-Literary Introduction,* Gottwald speaks of a contemporary "revolt," which has encouraged newer method.

> Religious and historical-critical schemes of biblical interpretation are widely perceived to have reached their limits on their own turf and to be inappropriate to clarifying major aspects of the Hebrew Bible that excite curiosity and imagination. On every hand one meets disappointment, restiveness, and a measure of resentment toward methods that promised so much but have insisted on exclusive billing long after they have made their best contributions. One may even speak of a widespread revolt against the tyranny of narrowly historical and religious methods of biblical study.[29]

New literary and sociological paradigms are cited as being important in the attempt to move beyond the present impasse. A literary paradigm emphasizes the Hebrew Bible "as a literary production that creates its own fictive world of meaning and is to be understood first and foremost, if not exclusively, as a literary medium, that is, as words that conjure up their own imaginative reality." The sociological paradigm, on the other hand, sees the Hebrew Bible "as a social document that reflects the history of changing social structures, functions, and roles in ancient Israel over a thousand years or so, and which provides an integral context in which the literary, historical, and religious features of the Israelite/Jewish people can be synoptically viewed and dynamically interconnected."[30]

A comprehensive approach to biblical texts that does justice to and harmonizes the literary and sociological methods is envisioned by Gottwald. Such an approach must not recapitulate the adversarial relationship between confessional and historical-critical methods. "If, on the one hand, literary critics insist that social context has no bearing on texts and if, on the other hand, anthropological and sociological critics claim that texts are pure and simple projections of social life and consciousness, it is likely that points of contact between them will be minimal at best and hostile at worst."[31] The correlation of the different methods is problematic. Gottwald questions whether the concept of structure might provide a means of harmonization.[32] Gottwald, however, betrays a nonstructural genetic bias. He says that "language itself as the medium of literature is a social code and thus literature is a social expression." He becomes more explicit in his genetic bias in the question: "Exactly how does social reality inscribe itself in language and in literary creations?"[33]

In a detailed analysis of the problem of the coordination of the literary and social dimensions following publication of his socio-literary introduction,[34] Gottwald develops the thesis that even though the different dimensions of biblical texts carry equal weight and imply their own methods for interpretation, they require one another for the interpretation of the fullness of the text. Beyond all of their disjunctions, there is a convergence of the literary, social, and theological worlds of the Bible, a convergence toward an horizon in which there is complementarity and mutuality, where all are simply aspects of a single biblical landscape.

> In the critical practices associated with the three coordinates are disclosed the simultaneous expressions of human beings who lived in communities of a certain social character and who wrote their thoughts and feelings in texts of certain types and who found meaning in their life together through religious categories of a specific sort. These literary, social and theological "worlds" which we split for analysis were inhabited by real people for whom those worlds were dimensions of their lived experience and shared meanings. The three coordinates which we are trying to bring together coexisted in their collective lives and interpreting minds, filtered through linguistic and cultural socialization processes.[35]

The desired synthesis of the literary and the social requires an advance beyond a caricature of New Criticism, which sees no relations of the text to extrinsic realities, and beyond a simplistic historicism, which explains the text as the result pure and simple of a historical "cause." Gottwald indicates that we must begin with the text as a whole, but we are not to "'reduce' everything to the closed world of the text." Opposition to the collapse of the meaning of the text "into a self-constituting structure impervious to the rest of life," however, does not take the form of making the text into "a mere veiled set of signs about exterior conditions and happenings." "The sui generis character of linguistic activity within the whole of human action must be respected and specified as a special way of rendering meaning that is in itself inseparable from the human life activities it refers to." A theory is necessary, therefore, which "explains how the widest realities of life generate meanings in the text, how the text is open in certain ways to penetration and formation by the limits and conditions of history, society and theology/ideology."[36]

Gottwald's vision is admirable and his coordination of the different aspects of biblical texts does advance study beyond simple historicist assumptions. For assistance in the achievement of a mutually helpful coordination of factors, Gottwald even uses the work of the literary critics Terry Eagleton and Fredric Jameson. Each of these scholars, however, begins with assumptions about the priority of the sociological-historical.

With Eagleton, a literary text "gives us certain socially determined representations of the real cut loose from any particular real conditions to which those representations refer." The text refers to an ideological formation produced by "concrete situations." The text gives us ideology without the underlying history. This free-wheeling imaginative appearance of the text is an illusion for Eagleton, who declares that "the function of criticism is to refuse the spontaneous presence of the work—to deny that 'naturalness' in order to make its real determinants appear."[37] Jameson's determinants are the "unresolvable social contradictions" that "cause" the imaginary "solutions" of fiction. The limits of an author's social and ideological world are mediated into the limit situations of literature.[38]

In the work of Gottwald, there is an assumption about the nature of the biblical text and the role of biblical study that not only helps to explain the appeal of Eagleton and Jameson, but also precludes the accomplishment of his vision. The task of study, for Gottwald, is the analysis of the literary, social, and theological "worlds" inhabited by those responsible for biblical literature. The unifying ground of the analysis "begins from and returns to the unifying ground of a people speaking, associating and generating religious meaning."

In Gottwald's approach, the three dimensions are only as coordinate as the historical paradigm allows. History, society, and ideology (in a secondary way) come out as dominant, as the literary "genetics." A structural conceptualization would emphasize meaning as a result of relationships within and among the various linguistic-literary, historical-social, and ideological-theological systems. A reader-oriented perspective would insist on the place of the actual reader in structures and the structuring process. If a genetic perspective is maintained, a genuine coordination of the various factors would conceive of the text, or language, as generating history—including the history of readers.

From a reader-oriented literary approach, then, contemporary sociological methods are to be seen as an advance on earlier sociologically unsophisticated historical methods but as remaining anchored in the same paradigm that has directed the historical-critical enterprise.

A Double Vision Approach

Attempts to give equal weight to historical criticism and theological reflection in a unified approach have made clear the impossibility of a simple foundationalist methodology. Different systems and different values are involved, resulting in bifurcation and often in antagonistic relationships between interdependent approaches. Some important oppositions are biblical interpretation in the university *versus* biblical interpretation in the church; historical exegesis *versus* theological exegesis; exegesis of the Bible as text *versus* exegesis of the Bible as scripture; and study of scripture as source *versus* study of scripture as canon.

Exegesis in the University and in the Church

Distinctions between university oriented and church oriented biblical interpretation were made in a series of essays in *Revue Biblique* in the late 1970s. In the essays, François Dreyfus made a clear distinction between exegesis in the Sorbonne and exegesis in the church, or exegesis conducted as a humanistic discipline and exegesis conducted as a churchly function. In the university, the Bible should be perceived as literature; in the church, the pastoral function is dominant, according to

Dreyfus. The aim of a university oriented literary science, in Dreyfus' opinion, is "to furnish the maximum of objective, communicable, verifiable elements" that can be used "for the purpose of appreciation of the masterpiece."[39] Even though the appreciation of the literary work of art goes beyond science, the engagement with the reader in literary criticism and appreciation is not the vital engagement that involves faith. Literary criticism and appreciation, then, do not deal with all that is involved in exegesis.

Dreyfus declares that it is essentially literary criticism's lack of capacity to deal with the object of the text, the pastoral object, that does not allow the study of the Bible to be reduced to literary science. Such study would be like reading the Ptolemaic texts on astronomy solely in the light of their literary aspect and ignoring the aim of the author. Historical and philosophical, as well as theological and ethical, aims and values are secondary in the literary criticism Dreyfus is discussing. This lack of ultimacy is seen by Dreyfus as an essential characteristic of literary criticism.

Dreyfus specifies three important differences in his distinction between exegesis in the Sorbonne and exegesis in the church. (1) Exegesis in the Sorbonne is that which studies the text under all of the aspects in which it can be an object of knowledge and uses all of the resources of human knowledge from the past. No hierarchy is established between the different aspects. Exegesis in the church, however, is limited to those aspects in which knowledge influences the content, the transmission, and the actualization of the message.

A hierarchy is established on the basis of the measure of influence the various aspects exercise. (2) Exegesis in the Sorbonne is exclusively rational, thus faith plays no part. Faith, however, is definitely involved in certain stages of exegesis in the church. (3) In exegesis in the Sorbonne, knowledge is its own end; exegesis is addressed to scholars and colleagues. In the church, exegesis has the end of serving the people of God. Independent exegesis as a humanistic discipline is comparable to the pure sciences; the dependent churchly exegesis is comparable to the applied sciences. It is concerned with serving the life and faith of the people of God.[40]

The pastoral finality of the text, stressed by Dreyfus, is not derived ultimately from the text itself but the text seen in relation to a larger context, the totality of scripture, and the traditions that actualize the text and the course of history of the people of God. In Dreyfus' view, then, the biblical text must be studied within the church to do full justice to its nature. This means that literary criticism, its principles, rules and results are to be utilized. "No area of the science of exegesis and the disciplines which it uses are without interest for exegesis in the church." The problem according to Dreyfus is to establish a hierarchy and to seek to distinguish the factors that are not significant for understanding the message from the factors upon which the message depends.[41]

Dreyfus' definition of the way the churchly situation affects interpretation takes cognizance of developments in hermeneutical theory and practice since the time of the ancient and medieval church, and his concern for the pastoral function to guide the perception of the reader is more in accord with contemporary world views than it is with the Neoplatonism of Augustine. The way Dreyfus frames the problem, therefore, may make *rapprochement* between university centered critical approaches and churchly approaches less problematic than he envisions in his articles. *Rapprochement,* of course, would result from a literary criticism that moved beyond a concept of the autonomy of the text to include extra-textual structures, including the needs and dynamic symbolic capacity of the reader. A literary criticism designed to supply objective, communicable, verifiable elements for the purpose of appreciation cannot deal well with the sacred—or with values the reader brings to the text, for that matter. A literary criticism that is reader centered, however, may reconceptualize the role and function of literature and criticism and develop disciplined ways of viewing the text as addressed to the entire person—intellect, sensibility, and sense of values. Such a view of literature and literary criticism does not exclude religious and ethical aspects, which are also aspects of the pastoral function with which Dreyfus is concerned. The question remains as to how the sacred may be envisioned from a literary perspective.

Dogmatics and Exegesis

Theological study and formulation is often thought of as depending on historical-critical exegesis. In fact, however, dogmatics and exegesis often go their own ways, each governed by presuppositions and objectives that are almost totally independent. In recent years, the relationship between dogmatics and exegesis has been restudied by theologians and biblical scholars, and the results of this study and reconceptualization are important for contemporary biblical study.

Dogmatic Historical Exegesis. Gerhard Ebeling has portrayed the relationship between dogmatics and exegesis as one marked by crisis and dissension. That impression of crisis is confirmed for Ebeling by the "history of theology of the last three centuries and a newly perceived *aporia* in light of the apparently hopelessly divergent disciplines."[42] Although Ebeling himself feels that a relative independence of exegesis and dogmatics is necessary, he also emphasizes that the exegesis of a text in the light of its subject matter (*Sachkritik*) must consciously participate in the dogmatic task. Interpretation must go beyond the purely historical event, not to make that event trivial, but to make it fruitful for the interpretation of the matter of the text. "Then the history does not become a hindrance in the task of interpretation but a mainspring."[43] In the context of hermeneutical responsibility, biblical criticism has the task of "letting the matter of the Bible come to light as clearly as possible against everything that tends to obscure and create misunderstanding, factors in the Bible as well as outside, factors on the side of the tradition or on the side of our own understanding of reality."[44]

Ebeling sees historical criticism as an adjunct of a hermeneutics in which consensus (*Einverständnis*) can arise. Consensus and historical criticism are not antithetical, however, for the central matter of the

Bible is not simply a thing to be grasped objectively in a formal way. The central matter of the Bible is such that its understanding is not separable from the event that conditions it.[45] A mark of historical criticism as normally practiced, however, is the definition of the aims and methods in such a way that question of consensus is not a factor. The descriptive historical study of the Bible and the study that Ebeling sees as the mainspring of a hermeneutical approach are quite different disciplines.

Exegesis of Historical Source Versus Exegesis of Scripture. The description Ebeling gives of a legitimate historical criticism is a historical criticism conceptualized in terms of Ebeling's own theological task. The "mainspring" of the theological task is not historical criticism as conceived and practiced by historical scholars. But no theologian uses historical criticism as the "mainspring" of theology, according to David H. Kelsey. The view of a theological position being built up piece by piece "as the several parts of the Bible are each studied by sophisticated critical methods and are then 'translated' into theological proposals cast in contemporary idiom, until the 'position' as a whole is completed" is a misunderstanding of what actually happens.[46] Theologians use the Bible within a framework that is not derived from the Bible. Decisions of theologians as to how to construe the scriptures are "decisively shaped by a theologian's prior judgment about how best to construe the mode in which God's presence among the faithful correlates with the use of scripture in the common life of the church."[47] Prior to theological formulation, a theologian engages in an "act of imagination" which "tries to catch up in a single metaphorical judgment the full complexity of God's presence in, through, and over-against the activities comprising the church's common life." In turn, this metaphorical judgment "provides the *discrimen* against which the theology criticizes the Church's current form of speech and life, and determines the peculiar 'shape' of the 'position.' "[48]

The theological use of the Bible, then, is as scripture construed in a certain way. Kelsey acknowledges that exegesis of biblical texts as text does influence this exegesis as scripture. By exegesis of texts as text, Kelsey means: (1) the study of a text as a historical source, which itself has historical sources, and (2) the study of the text as it now stands, a study that assumes that the writing is to be understood in the light of the intention that shaped the work for its original audience in its original context.[49] Exegesis of biblical texts as text has influenced the exegesis of biblical texts as scripture in two ways, in the opinion of Kelsey. Historically, such exegesis seems "to have exercised a certain amount of psychological influence on theologians' imaginative and reasoned elaboration of biblical patterns" and thereby to have aided the Christian community to transcend *status quo* opinions prevalent at particular times. It has also "set limits to what may be asserted historically and literarily about biblical passages" and played a role in arguments made on behalf of theological proposals. Limits have been set because arguments "have to conform to what can be established by normal methods of historical or literary-critical arguments."[50] Exegesis of biblical texts as text, however, does not have a normative function in doing theology. Kelsey's work suggests that, in fact, there is an exegesis of the Bible that is carried out according to the canons of *historical* rationality and another that is carried out according to the canons of *theological* rationality and construction. It is instructive to note that historical and theological methods correlate to historical rationality on the one hand and to theological rationality on the other hand. The interdependence of method and ideology, however, obviously crosses over historical and theological lines, with the canons of historical rationality being related to theological construction and canons of theological rationality being related to historical elaboration.

Scripture as Source and Scripture as Canon. A contemporary way of distinguishing historical study from dogmatic construction is to distinguish between scripture as source and scripture as canon. Charles M. Wood has described this method of conceiving the different approaches. As source, "Scripture is the repository of the formative traditions of the community. . . . The discovery and exhibition of the varied contents of this resource by every means available is a continuing task, essential to the health of the community." The study of the texts as they stand and as compilations of earlier sources involves breaking the text "out of its canonical context" and restoring it "to the context of its historical development, its *Sitz im Leben,* where it may take on quite a different sense." Wood acknowledges that "there can be no doubt that our present knowledge of primitive Christianity and of the history of Israel has been enormously enriched through such critical-historical study."

The study of scripture as canon, however, is not the same as the study of scripture as source. The canonization of Christian scripture is seen by Wood as "the bestowal upon these texts of a specific function." The drawing of margins around the particular texts "establishes new relationships among them, and between them and extracanonical Christian tradition, past, contemporary, and future." The texts as canon are "understood and used as a criterion of Christian witness, as a standard by which the 'traditioning' activity of the Christian community is to be critically assessed and directed."[51]

Both approaches are necessary, and one should not be subsumed by the other. "It is not the aim of the study of scripture as source either to vindicate or to supplant the use of scripture as canon, any more than it is the role of scripture as canon to direct or to challenge its study as source." Nevertheless the Christian use of scripture as source is governed by scripture as canon. Wood's conceptualization shows clearly the interdependence of theological and historical presuppositions or ideologies and methods in his insistence that theological considerations may govern the historical study of texts. As source, the Bible is seen as "an assemblage of greatly differing strategies for recollecting, interpreting, and sharing the community's witness concerning God. They defy harmonization. They do clash. It is impossible . . . to affirm them all simultaneously." The church can use this material because it makes judgments "in the light of the canon itself, as to the Christianness of some of its components, individually considered. . . . Scripture as canon must rule the Christian use of scripture as source."[52]

An Apology for a Literary Approach to the Biblical Text

Limitations of the Constantinian Paradigm

The horizon against which the various critical and theological positions and approaches have been understood and applied is that of the ancient and medieval church, which has constrained the appreciation of the biblical text. The cognitive function of the text has been assumed as the paramount, if not the exclusive, function. The cognitive horizon of the ancient and medieval church practically precluded a movement back to the more affective horizon of the Hebrew scriptures and the New Testament themselves. Augustine noted the delight in the use of figurative language, but he quickly disavowed any real value in the figures because of his assumption that the biblical text was to convey dogmatic and ethical information. Charles S. McCoy speaks of the pattern prevailing since the time of Augustine as the "Constantinian paradigm." With variations, this paradigm "has dominated Christian thought in the West since the time of Augustine. Thomas Aquinas followed this pattern. The Reformers continued it with revisions. Schleiermacher and Barth, Bultmann and Rahner adhere to it, as do most persons working in theological faculties of the North Atlantic nations." The Bible is studied in terms of some type of philosophical system within the context of institutional Christianity. Theological statements, moreover, are proclaimed in the imperial mode. "Faith is turned into some kind of knowledge, and the believer is turned into God."[53]

The revolt of Protestant reformers against medieval Catholicism resulted only in variation of the traditional paradigm. Most Protestant theology also depends on philosophy, and "even that which explicitly rejected philosophy in favor of the Bible still followed the traditional paradigm in using a rationally discursive form for theological discourse."[54] The role and function of the Bible, then, has been limited by the cognitive theological framework within which biblical study and interpretation have taken place. The importance of the affective functions of scripture and the role of various literary genres as parable, story, and saga have been eclipsed by the stress on dogmatic formulations consistent with philosophical notions of truth.

The historical-critical approach has not radically altered theological use of the Bible at a formal level. The historical-critical approach has served a vital function in providing some limits to theological formulation, but it has not provided normative direction in that formulation. The historical and theological frames of conceptualizations are not valueless, but they are limitations when they constrain the reader in viewing the text and its meaning in a way that separates the text and its meaning from life. The "scientific" operations governed by critical historical and theological conceptualizations and methods do not suffice for contemporary readers. Is it possible to conceptualize a contemporary framework for biblical study that utilizes the critical insights and strategies in an appropriate fashion to relate the text and its meaning to the lives of readers? It is the thesis of this book that a dynamic framework may be conceptualized on the basis of contemporary reader centered approaches to literature. For contemporary readers and critics to become convinced of the possibilities of a reader-oriented approach, we must be disabused of existing views of literary ideologies, and we must be convinced that such a literary approach is not inconsistent with the nature of the biblical text.

A Literary Paradigm for the Bible

Is the nature of the biblical text consistent with a literary approach? The question is not whether the writings are literary masterpieces, judged according to literary standards of this or any other era. Biblical writings plainly were not composed within "literary" circles, nor were they designed to be read simply for enjoyment as "literary" works of art. The writings stem from religious communities and have functions consistent with those communities. Ideas about literature, growing out of Romanticism, would preclude consideration of biblical writings as genuine literature. These ideas concern the specific or exclusive nature of literature: A literary work of art is fundamentally different from other uses of language. The reality of literature is a world of its own. Literature, then, is essentially independent of historical, social, and economic realities. Its value and meaning are not determined historically. Its products and reception are transcendent of any specific environment. Associated with this idea is the notion that the production and reception of literature are mystical, transcendent phenomena and that the uniqueness of the literary work is fully grasped only by an irrational "understanding."[55] The aim of literary study is to explain why a particular work of art is beautiful.

Judged in the light of these literary ideologies, the Bible could not be approached as literature. But these ideologies are no longer self-evident in literary criticism. All sorts of texts may be read as literature, regardless of their original functions. The question now is: *Can* the Bible be read as literature? Here we are closer to a satisfying answer, if we do not subscribe to the limited view of literary evaluation mentioned earlier. Biblical texts are linguistic structures. The same linguistic and literary principles at work in the case of literary masterpieces are at work in the case of biblical writings. Readers can also come to the biblical text and exercise their creative imaginations. A rich difference of opinion exists today over the relative importance of the text and the reader and the best ways of conceptualizing the activities of the reader in actualizing the text. But there is unanimity of opinion that the reader is necessarily and legitimately involved in the process of reading.

Kelsey has shown convincingly that creative imagination is basic in the activity of theologians. The "imaginative construal" of the theologian is the "basis of assessments of theological proposals and the 'theological positions' they comprise."[56]

David Tracy emphasizes the reader's imagination in the latter stages of the theological enterprise. Earlier stages include the historical (in which the texts are reconstructed), the semantic (in which the linguistic structures of the images and symbols involved in the text are determined), and the literary-critical (in which the literary genres are determined, the genres by means of which the images, metaphors, and symbols are structured, codified, and transformed). For Tracy, the imagination is involved primarily in the hermeneutical task of explicating the referent. The referent is distinct from the sense gained from the internal structure or the historical reconstruction. The referent is the meaning "in front of" the text, "that way of perceiving reality, that mode of being-in-the-world which the text opens up for the intelligent reader." The possible way of being-in-the-world is "a project for our imagination to envision."[57] As we shall see later, Tracy's stages must be seen not as distinct but as interdependent, and the imaginative activity of the reader must be seen as involved in all stages. Nevertheless Tracy's conceptualization is consistent with a reader-oriented approach to biblical literature and introduces the question of the sort of meaning appropriate for a literary approach.

Theological and Literary Meaning

Normally, the model for interpretation of the biblical text is drawn from "scientific" communication, in which the object of communication is a reality that is uncovered by logical investigation. The reference is to something in the real world, and the reader makes sense of the text by matching the object in the text with the object in the real world. Historical study uses this model; conventional theology also uses this approach with the exception that the object is in the real world of logical, philosophical, and theological conceptualizations. From a contemporary perspective, the Bible cannot be reduced to a collection of documents referring to historical events or theological concepts that are discovered by historical and theological methods. The biblical text may be seen as essentially an appeal for the reader's capacity for imagination and need for meaning that coheres with the reader's own situation in the world.

The biblical writings do grow out of particular historical contexts. Biblical writers actually referred directly, as well as obliquely, to events and ideas in the real world, and these events and ideas may be uncovered to some extent by appropriate methods. A literary approach to the Bible in the context of contemporary literary study, however, allows—even requires—a view of the text as both an ancient document with original meaning and a living message with contemporary significance. The text *referred* not simply to facts but also to realities to be construed by the readers in their situation (ancient readers as well as modern readers). At times, this distinction is made by speaking of a meaning intended by the author and a significance construed by the reader. But do creative authors not *intend* that readers construe a significance that involves their own capacities and needs? Involved in the meaning, then would be a significance to be construed by the reader.

The creative use of traditional sources by the communities of Israel and the early church show that they discerned the significance and were able to distinguish between some original verbal meaning and the meaning the author intended readers to construct for themselves. This is part of the explanation of the richness for present day readers and also a pattern for contemporary methods of making sense. Historical study, concerned with recovering the most original sources of the history of Israel or the authentic words of Jesus, tends to look at the development of the tradition as a progressive falsification of the data, which must be discounted. It is possible to see the development of tradition as a dynamic matching of the literary tradition with the needs and capacities of later readers. Sense was made of the "events" of Israel and Jesus Christ by succeeding generations so that their meaning and significance were extended and made available in the later tradition. The story of Jesus was told and retold, written and rewritten, so as to make sense of Jesus for the speakers/writers and their audiences. In later contexts, the church made sense intellectually and emotionally through theological and historical construction and reconstruction. Because of the world views within which the Church made sense of the Bible, however, the biblical text came to be limited to a message that could be extracted.

Today, we may find satisfaction in returning in some measure to the pattern of the religious communities out of which scripture developed. We may not only appreciate the multiplicity of ways of telling and hearing of biblical traditions that helped the earlier tellers and hearers make sense for their lives, but we may also use the traditions to make sense for ourselves. We need not deny historical events and theological truths independent of the biblical text to affirm that the texts are more than containers of such information. We may come to the texts with a variety of needs and capacities and discover an overflow of meaning and significance in the texts as literature.

Notes

1. Contemporary movements in biblical studies result in part from the attempt to provide for biblical studies what Hans Robert Jauß says is a requirement for literary studies: "The capacity to rescue works of art from the past by means of continually new interpretations, to transfer them into a new presence, to make the experience preserved in past art once more available, in other words: to ask questions—which must be discovered by each new generation—questions to which the art of the past can respond for us once again." (Hans Robert Jauß, "Paradigmawechsel in der Literaturwissenschaft," *Linguistiche Berichte* 3 [1969]:54-56.).

2. Alan Richardson, "The Rise of Modern Biblical Scholarship and Recent Discussion of the Authority of the Bible," in *Cambridge History of the Bible*, vol. 3, "The West from the Reformation to the Present Day," ed. S. L. Greenslade (Cambridge, England: Cambridge University Press, 1963), p. 304.

3. Ibid., p. 314.

4. Ibid., pp. 302-3.

5. The liberal view of the human capacity had altered. In Europe, "dialectical theology" had emphasized that people do not know God as an object; an absolute gulf exists between humans and God that God alone can bridge. God, then, is known only as subject acting upon humans, not as an object of our scrutiny.

6. He was aware that objectivity was a myth for past scholars. "We can smile when we see how an earlier generation of biblical scholars peddled Kantian, Hegelian or Ritschlian ideas, all the time subjectively convinced that they themselves were objective scholars who only stated 'facts.'" He was

convinced, nevertheless, that objectivity was no myth in the mid-twentieth century. A program of objective description was now possible. "Such a program is by and large a new feature in biblical studies, a mature fruit of the historical method." The descriptive task regarding the biblical texts, which Stendahl is confident can be carried out, is "to find out what these words meant when uttered or written by the prophet, the priest, the evangelist, or the apostle—and regardless of their meaning in later stages of religious history, our own included" (Krister Stendahl, "Contemporary Biblical Theology," in *The Interpreter's Dictionary of the Bible*, vol. 1 [Nashville: Abingdon Press, 1962], p. 422).

7. Ibid., pp. 428-29, 431.

8. James Barr, "Revelation Through History in the Old Testament and in Modern Theology," *Interpretation* 17 (1963):193-205. Barr's accurate and compelling criticism that historical-critical study of the Bible did not establish the meta-historical framework used by biblical theology for understanding biblical texts was not accompanied by a positive alternative such as that which could have been provided by some of his linguistic insights. Biblical texts and meanings are to be understood in relationship but not in any relationship governed by evolutionary historical ideologies. Within the Hebrew Bible, for example, the various sorts of approaches (Torah, Wisdom, Prophecy) are not simply to be understood in progressive sequence. Texts representing the various traditions are to be interpreted in the light of these traditions and in the light of texts from other traditions. The meanings discerned are all temporally and culturally conditioned, but the meanings are not essentially derived from the temporal or cultural settings. Meanings are not discerned by being judged as early or late in a developmental scheme.

9. Brevard S. Childs, *Introduction to the Old Testament as Scripture* (Philadelphia: Fortress Press, 1979), p. 73.

10. Ibid.

11. James A. Sanders, *Torah and Canon* (Philadelphia: Fortress Press, 1972), p. xvii.

12. James A. Sanders, *Canon and Community: A Guide to*

Canonical Criticism, Guides to Biblical Scholarship series (Philadelphia: Fortress Press, 1984), pp. 8-9.

13. James A. Sanders, "Hermeneutics," in *The Interpreter's Dictionary of the Bible*, supplementary vol. (Nashville: Abingdon Press, 1976), p. 403.

14. Ibid., pp. 403-4.

15. Sanders, *Canon and Community*, p. 19.

16. Childs, *Introduction to the Old Testament as Scripture*, p. 77.

17. Ibid., p. 79.

18. Ibid.

19. Rudolf Bultmann, *The History of the Synoptic Tradition*, trans. John Marsh (New York: Harper, 1961), p. 205.

20. Peter Stuhlmacher, *Vom Verstehen des Neuen Testament: Eine Hermeneutik*, Grundrisse zum Neuen Testament, vol. 6 (Göttingen: Vandenhoeck & Ruprecht, 1st ed. 1979; 2nd ed. 1986).

21. Adolf Schlatter, *Das Christliche Dogma*, 2nd ed. (Stuttgart: Calwer Verlag, 1923), p. 375.

22. Adolf Schlatter, "Ätheistische Methoden in der Theologie," in *Zur Theologie des Neuen Testaments and zur Dogmatik: Kleine Schriften mit einer Einfuhrung*, ed. U. Luck (Munich: Chr. Kaiser Verlag, 1969), pp. 142-43.

23. See Peter Stuhlmacher, *Historical Criticism and Theological Interpretation of Scripture: Towards a Hermeneutics of Consent*, trans. Roy A. Harrisville (Philadelphia: Fortress Press, 1977), p. 46.

24. Schlatter, "Ätheistische Methoden in der Theologie," pp. 148-49.

25. Stuhlmacher, *Vom Verstehen des Neuen Testament*, 1st ed., p. 206; 2nd ed., p. 223. Hereafter referred to in the text as *VVNT*.

26. While the Bible serves as more than a historical collection, Stuhlmacher did not advocate a special hermeneutics for faith since the original historical purpose seen through

historical research is consent (*Einverständnis*) to the biblical text. The purpose of the text may be carried out whether one is concerned with information as historical knowledge or information related to faith, because the texts were written originally for the purpose of giving an understandable report about Jesus' messianic work of reconciliation and engendering belief in him for those seeking information and direction. The answer of the text, then, is directed to believer and nonbeliever to the same degree. Hermeneutics must not assume belief as a principle of understanding; it must be satisfied to give an account concerning its texts in the greatest possible honesty and clarity (*VVNT*, pp. 218-19).

27. Stuhlmacher, *Vom Verstehen des Neuen Testament*, pp. 229-30. Stuhlmacher explicitly related his work of theological reconstruction as well as his reformulation of method to the work of Schlatter: "A. Schlatter's major question to liberal biblical criticism, if the earthly Jesus must not be understood historically as the Messiah, is to be once again confronted and . . . to be answered affirmatively" (*VVNT*, p. 247).

28. Norman K. Gottwald, *The Hebrew Bible: A Socio-Literary Introduction* (Philadelphia: Fortress Press, 1985), pp. 28-29.

29. Ibid., p. 21.

30. Ibid., p. 22.

31. Ibid., p. 30.

32. He suggests that "if structural criticism of texts presupposes a constantly structured and structuring human mind . . . sociological data will at least appear as instances of this unitary mind at work, parallel in a sense with literary instances of that mind. This outlook could provide a harmonizing of the two kinds of structures" (ibid., pp. 30-31).

33. Ibid., p. 31.

34. Norman K. Gottwald, "Literary Criticism of the Hebrew Bible: Retrospect and Prospect" (paper delivered to the Section on Biblical Criticism and Literary Criticism at the national meeting of the Society of Biblical Literature, November 24, 1986).

35. Ibid., p. 4.

36. Ibid., p. 12.

37. Terry Eagleton, *Criticism and Ideology: A Study of Marxist Literary Theory* (London: New Left Books, 1976), pp. 73-74, 101. Cited favorably in Gottwald, "Literary Criticism of the Hebrew Bible," p. 13.

38. Fredric Jameson, *The Political Unconscious: Narratives as a Socially Symbolic Act* (Ithaca, N.Y.: Cornell University Press, 1981), pp. 35, 79, 102. Cited in Gottwald, "Literary Criticism of the Hebrew Bible," p. 14.

39. F. Dreyfus, "Exégèse en Sorbonne, Exégèse en Eglise," *Revue Biblique* 81 (1975):321-59.

40. Ibid., pp. 337-38.

41. He suggests a mathematical formulation of the problem. If y is the message of the text, which is determined by $x, x_2 \ldots x_n$, the different elements that could contribute to the establishment of the message (all the stages of exegetical research, the contributions of related disciplines), it is necessary to determine if a modification of the different variables $(x_1 \ldots x_n)$ would modify y. It is necessary in the function $y = f\ (x, x_2 \ldots x_n)$ to study the partially derived y prime (x_n). If it is 0, the element considered xn is not significant for the elucidation of the message. Ibid., p. 330, n. 17.

42. Gerhard Ebeling, "Dogmatik und Exégèse," *Zeitschrift für Theologie und Kirche* 77 (1980):269-70.

43. Ibid., p. 286.

44. Ibid., p. 272.

45. Ibid., p. 274.

46. David H. Kelsey, *The Uses of Scripture in Recent Theology* (Philadelphia: Fortress Press, 1975), p. 159.

47. Ibid., p. 167.

48. Ibid., p. 163.

49. Ibid., p. 198.

50. Ibid., pp. 199-200.

51. Charles M. Wood, *The Formation of Christian Understanding: An Essay in Theological Hermeneutics* (Philadelphia: The Westminster Press, 1981), pp. 87-88, 90-91.

52. Ibid., pp. 89-90, 105.

53. Charles S. McCoy, *When Gods Change: Hope for Theology* (Nashville: Abingdon Press, 1980), pp. 25-26, 29.

54. Ibid., p. 113.

55. Teun A. Van Dijk, "Advice on Theoretical Poetics," *Poetics* 8 (1979):577-79.

56. Kelsey, *The Uses of Scripture in Recent Theology*, p. 215.

57. David Tracy, *Blessed Rage for Order: The New Pluralism in Theology*, the Seabury Library of Contemporary Theology (New York: Seabury Press, 1979), pp. 50-52, 78.

Chapter Three

Literary Perspectives and Resources for Postmodern Use:

Structures, Codes, and the Reader

Structure in the sense of relationship or connection is vital in literature. Words and sentences themselves constitute sets of relationships of meaning and sentences come together in different ways to form patterns of meaning beyond the sentence. For structures to communicate meaning, there must be shared conventions or codes. The structuralist tradition in literary study has, therefore, emphasized the relationship of linguistic and literary structures to cultural codes or conventions. In the process of communication, moreover, the ordering or structuring is an activity involving the individual as well as the text and society. The examination of structures, cultural codes, and the role of the individual reader in this chapter will emphasize the interdependence of the three factors in the process of reading and interpretation. This chapter may be seen as the translation of the assumptions of an antifoundationalist approach to knowledge into the area of language and literature, for both approaches see knowledge and meaning in terms of relationships within and between systems and in terms of life and experience.

Structure

The term *structure* is used in a variety of ways. It refers to linguistic and literary relationships within units, and it refers to the superior units that result from those relationships. Structures are ascertained in view of actual existing texts (surface level) and in view of abstract (or deep level) relationships, which are seen as determining the structures on the surface level. What is common in all of the views of structure is the importance of relationship. A particular linguistic or literary element has meaning and significance in terms of the relationships it has with other linguistic and literary units in the system under consideration and in terms of its relationships with other systems.

This section will begin with a discussion of the basic insights of structural linguistics that are responsible for the structural "revolution" and will show how these insights influence literary interpretation. The New Critical view of the literary text is then discussed in the light of the structuralist conceptualization.

Structures in the Structural Tradition

French structuralism's depreciation of individual valuation and reduction of culture and the individual to formal codes—to binary oppositions in the case of Claude Lévi-Strauss—has innoculated many against genuine values to be found in the broader structural tradition. The basic tenets of structural linguistics and their early application in literary study may give help in the present philosophical and literary context.

Structural Linguistics. The formalist-structuralist tradition parallels the New Critical tradition in its emphasis on the study of the text as a linguistic-literary unity. Insights from various streams of this tradition have transformed literary studies, but all may be seen as flowing from four fundamental dichotomies in structural linguistics: synchronic/diachronic, language-system (*langue*)/language in use (*parole*), signified/signifier, and syntagmatic/associative.

The emphasis on synchrony rather than diachrony and the system of language (*langue*) rather than its use (*parole*) changed the focus of the study of linguistics from the evolutionary oriented study of particular instances of language to the study of the language system as it exists at a particular moment in time. This is translated into literary studies as a concern with the text as it exists in its canonical form and is the result of linguistic and literary relationships, rather than a concern with the historical antecedents of the text and its historical relationships.

Structural linguistics' view of value or meaning in language is given in the dichotomy signified/signifier. A linguistic sign is not to be conceived as the relationship or "contract" between a word and an object in the world outside language. Rather a sign is the relationship between a "signifier," or sound image (an arbitrary division of the abstract sound spectrum), and a "signified," or concept (an arbitrary division of a conceptual field). The sign (the basic unit of communication that exists within the language system of a community), then, is arbitrary in that there is no objective, natural, or inevitable link between the signifier and the signified. (An exception exists in the case of onomatopoeia, of course.) The signifier represented by *cat* could be replaced by any other sequence of sounds if it were accepted by the speech community.

Syntagmatic and Associative Structures. The terms *syntagmatic* and *associative* refer to the two major types of relationships existing between signs. A proper understanding of the mutuality of these types of relationships will show how attention may be given at the same time to relationships within any given linguistic/literary unit and to relationships of that unit with other systems. Syntagmatic and associative relationships may be understood and illustrated conveniently on the level of words and sentences related to discourse. Syntagmatic relationships are relationships *within* discourse. "In discourse . . . words acquire relations based on the linear nature of language because they are chained together. . . . In the syntagm a term acquires its value only because it stands in opposition to everything that precedes or follows it, or to both."[1] In the sentence *John runs,* a syntagmatic relationship exists between the noun *John* and the verb *runs.* This same relationship exists between any two words, the first of which can serve as subject to the second. Syntagmatic relationships help define a word, because the differences between the word and other words in an acceptable sentence are crucial in the definition of a word.

Associative relations are those *outside* discourse. They are not supported by linearity; rather, "they are a part of the inner storehouse that makes up the language of each speaker."[2] Words that have something in common "are associated in the memory, resulting in groups marked by diverse relations." For each of the many types of relation, there is an associative series. The word *teaching*, for example, will be associated in memory with numerous other words on the basis of meaning—*teach, acquaint, education, apprenticeship,* and other related words. All of these relationships are essential in the sense that if one of the words lost some such relationships and gained others, the word would lose its old identity. For example, if *education* was not a word, the word *teaching* would change its identity in a subtle way. The basis (the organizing principle) of the associative series is not limited to lexical meaning. Bases may be such things as the root that is common to a number of different words, a common suffix, the similarity of the sound image, and the analogy of the concepts signified. One word enters into numerous associative series.

Structural linguistics also speaks of associative relationships of a word in paradigmatic or grammatical terms. These are relationships a word has with all of the words that could replace it in a sentence without making the sentence unacceptable (words of the same class, in the same case, and so on). In the sentence *John runs,* the verb *runs* could be replaced by numerous other verbs, such as *moves, flees,* and *hastens.* All of the paradigmatic relationships of a word (all of the words that could be used in place of the verb *run,* for example) are important in determining the formal identity of that word.[3]

The different relationships of units of a building illustrate syntagmatic and associative relationships.

> A linguistic unit is like a fixed part of a building, e.g. a column. On the one hand, the column has a certain relation to the architrave that it supports; the arrangement of the two units in space suggests the syntagmatic relation. On the other hand, if the column is Doric, it suggests a mental comparison of this style with others (Ionic, Corinthian, etc.) although none of these elements is present in space: the relation is associative.[4]

The associative relationships are multiple. An analysis of all of the associative series in which a given word falls would be virtually endless. In the act of discourse, naturally, all possibilities are not entertained consciously by speaker and hearer, only those possibilities that make sense in the particular situation of communication.

Associative Relationships and Semiotics. Application of structural linguistics following French structuralism gave attention primarily to paradigmatic linguistic and literary categories rather than to associative series, with their various meanings and significations. Interest today is not only in the abstract structures but also in the particular literary functions and meanings carried out and conveyed by the structures and their content. Such an interest may be served by paralleling the concept of associative series with semiotics' idea of interpretants. The concept of interpretant comes from Charles S. Peirce, who claimed that the three fundamental conceptions in semiotics are reference to a ground, reference to an object, and reference to an interpretant. (He called these "icons," "indices," and "symbols.") With "icons" or "indices" the representation is grounded in some likeness or correspondence in fact. With "symbols," the ground of the relation of representations to objects is imputed. It is this third type with which the interpretant is associated.[5] We are not to equate Saussure's signified and signifier with Peirce's object and sign. The sign, for Saussure, is the combination of signified and signifier, which is a fixed bond with respect to the community that uses it even though it is not a timeless "contract."[6] It is the sign (conceived of by the community as a fixed entity) which participates in word families (associative series) and thereby gains its value.

The fact that for structural linguistics the same sign or term fits into different associative units is related to the fact that for semiotics a particular unit may have different interpretants. In something of the same way that a term is involved in many associative series, the interpretant can assume different forms—the equivalent sign in another system of communication, an established connotation resulting from an emotive association, the translation of the term into another language, an index directed to the single object that implies universal quantification, a scientific definition in terms of the same system of communication.[7] The interpretant, then, is whatever the sign is capable of determining. In broad terms, the interpretant is the meaning of the sign, which in turn may become a sign with its own interpretant.[8]

Literary Structuralism. In the application of structural linguistics to literature, the view is taken that the entire linguistic system can be reduced to a theory of syntagmatic and associative relations. The same sorts of relationships that exist on the level of language exist also on the level of literature. "Our memory holds in reserve all the more or less complex types of syntagms, regardless of their class or length, and we bring in the associative groups to fix our choice when the time for using them arrives."[9] The syntagmatic/associative dichotomy may easily be translated into a combination/selection dichotomy (or axis) with literary creation being reduced to the two basic processes of combination and selection.

> If "child" is the topic of the message, the speaker selects one among the extant, more or less similar, nouns like child, kid, youngster, tot, all of them equivalent in a certain respect, and then, to comment on this topic, he may select one of the semantically cognate verbs—sleeps, dozes, nods, naps. Both chosen words combine in the speech chain. The selection is produced on the basis of equivalence, similarity and dissimilarity, synonymity and antonymity, while the combination, the build up of the sequence, is based on contiguity.[10]

Different functions of the text affect the selection (the associative axis). What is important at one time may be the referential (denotative, cognitive) function. Authors of scientific texts give primary attention to selection of terms that will be understood precisely by the addressee. At other times, the speaker's attitude toward the topic being discussed (the emotive function) is to be seen as primary in the choice of terms. The conative function (having to do with the will of the addressee) is often dominant. At times the phatic function (concerned with maintaining the contact between the addresser and the addressee) is involved. The metalingual function (as indicted by the word) has to do with language about language. Emphasis is then on the code that enables communication to take place.

The poetic function focuses on the message for its own sake, and with this function the relationship of selection to combination is unique—at the opposite end of the spectrum from the referential function. Equivalence in meaning is the principle that operates on the axis of selection when the referential function is dominant. In the illustration above, the noun *kid* could be selected because it is equivalent in meaning to *child*. With the poetic function, the principle of equivalence becomes the constitutive device not only of selection but also of the sequence (the axis of combination). "The poetic function projects the principle of equivalence from the axis of selection into the axis of combination." This is obvious with sound in poetry. The secondary poetic function of the political slogan "I like Ike" is effective because equivalence in sound has become the constitutive principle of the sequence. The basis for selection (or "frame"), insofar as the poetic function is concerned, is sound, but this is also the basis for combination. (Of course, the selection of words in the slogan is also influenced by conventional meanings of words because the poetic function is not primary.)[11]

The assumption that different levels of language and literature operate according to the same principles of selection and combination (selection from associative groups to fit into different types of syntagms) makes analysis of literary structure complex. Attention must be given to associative and syntagmatic relationships throughout the text. Syntagmatic relationships are most obvious. Words come together to form sentences, and sentences come together in various ways to form paragraphs, which then combine to form complete literary works. Associative relationships are more difficult to conceptualize.

In illustrations from Saussure and Jakobson, it has been observed that the proper selection of a word in a sentence is possible only when a particular syntagmatic organization is posited. A particular word in a sentence has value or meaning only in relation to the entire sentence and its function and value or meaning. We may think of a syntagm in general in terms of both its "form" and "content" and use the terms *frame* and *topic* to designate formal and informational characteristics. As we relate literary elements to meaning in terms of theme or topic, we also relate them to grammatical-type categories (genre at the level of a completed work, for example). In fact, the formal category and informational content are interdependent, but in general the formal, or generic aspect is conceived as more basic, and the topic guides the amalgamation at a conscious level. But where does the topic come from? In discourse, it may be obvious from the situation shared by the speaker and the hearer. In literature, however, it comes from the larger literary complex. Frames and topics on the lower level are in a dialectical relationship with frames and topics on higher levels.

In the larger literary work, a sentence (or a group of sentences) must be conceived of as carrying out the same function as does the word in the sentence.

Therefore, the sentence, or group of sentences, enters into more comprehensive syntagmatic and associative relationships. Take, for example, Luke 5:1, "While the people pressed upon him to hear the word of God, he was standing by the lake of Gennesaret." What is the organizing principle of this sentence? It is only as Luke 5:1-3 is seen as a complete elementary narrative unit that the portion 5:1 can be assigned a topic or function. Luke 5:1-3 may be seen as a unit, depicting activities to enable Jesus to escape from the press of the crowd and to carry out the objective of teaching the Word of God.

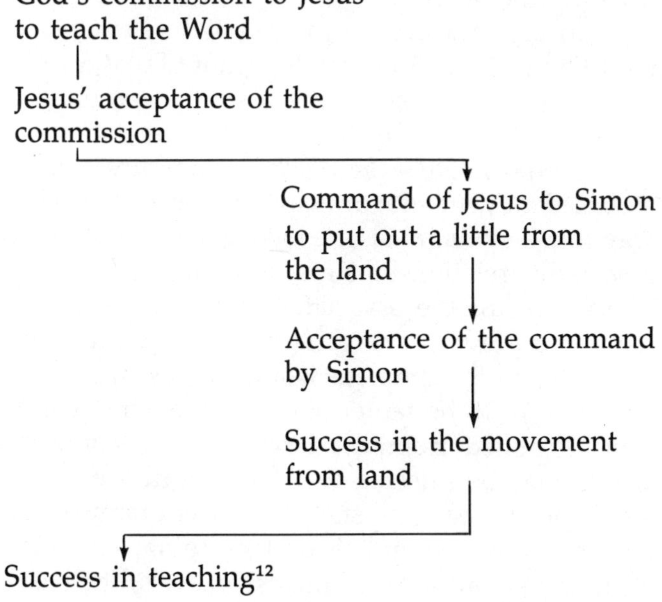

Jesus requests that Simon put the boat out a little from the land. Simon accepts this request, and this is followed by success in the teaching of Jesus.

But the elementary narrative of Luke 5:1-3 is, in fact, part of a larger narrative complex. A more inclusive analysis must begin with the action of the sending of Jesus by God for the purpose of teaching the Word of God. This is implied in Luke 5:1-11 itself, although it is clearly stated in the material immediately preceding the narrative (Luke 4:43). Luke 5:1-3 is an enclave narrative sequence, allowing movement from Jesus' acceptance of the commission to teach the Word to success in teaching the Word.

An inclusive structural analysis of the elementary narrative of Luke 5:1-3 cannot ignore Luke 5:1-11. But a proper analysis of this narrative eventually requires all of the Gospel of Luke—and more.

Structures Beyond the Work. In literature, analysis based on structural principles proceeds in such a way that a syntagm at one level enters into sets of associative relationships at a more inclusive level. The nature of the associative series depends, in part, on the level of analysis (sentence, narrative or discourse unit, complete work, corpus of works, and so on). At the sentence level (with a frame and topic supplied from the larger literary context), words may be selected for inclusion in the linear series on the basis of such things as grammatical considerations, sound, lexical meaning, connotation, and so on. In more inclusive levels, the basis for selection (with a frame and topic supplied from a yet more inclusive literary context) may be the category of the narrative or didactic unit (corresponding to the class or case relationship on the sentence level) or the nature of the represented action, character, object, environment, and so on.

At the level of the total literary work, the question of frame and topic is problematic from the structuralist perspective. One way to continue with the structuralist program is to consider the particular work as one unit in a syntagm that includes other units (works by the same author, works of the same period, and so on). In some fashion, a comprehensive organizing principle or "idea" must be formulated in order for the identification of structures throughout the work. This idea does not arise out of the structures of the work itself. If it is not developed by consciously placing the work in a larger context, the idea must be intuited.

Roman Ingarden speaks of the comprehensive idea of a work being "revealed." Ingarden's concept of the organization and meaning of a literary work of art is very much like the dynamic structural perspective proposed here. The totality of the "represented objects" of a literary work may be thought of as the "world" of the work. Ingarden emphasizes that the objects, persons, and so on in the literary text are *represented;* they result from a creative artistic imagination. The "represented objects," therefore, must be viewed from some perspective or through some cognitive filter. A distinction is made between the world of the literary work, which must be imaged, and the "idea," which may be conceived on the basis of the work.[13]

The comprehensive idea that is revealed is not directly a result of the literary work itself. It is the result of the level of "metaphysical qualities," which exists at least potentially for literary works. When metaphysical qualities are experienced by a reader, this level—and not the strata of sound, subordinate meaning units, represented objects, or schematized aspects (cognitive filter)—becomes the "core" of the literary work by means of which the "deeper sense" of life and existence is revealed or even by which the usually hidden "sense of life" is constituted.

It is instructive to keep in mind the concept of some overarching associative series when we consider Ingarden's "idea," or "core."

> The "idea" of the literary work of art is a "demonstrated," synthetic, essential complex of mutually modulated, aesthetically valent qualities which is brought to concrete appearance either in the work or by means of it. The aesthetically valent qualities lead to the intuitive constitution of a certain aesthetic value, and this value forms a whole, in intimate unity, with the basis on which it is founded (the literary work of art itself).[14]

Wolfgang Iser speaks of a "basic force" or "frame" within which relevant material of a particular literary text is organized and subsumed. He calls this force "negativity." It is the unformulated "double" or "background" to which "practically all the formulations of the text refer"; the "unwritten base," which conditions the formulations of the text by way of blanks and negation; and the "reverse side of the represented world."[15] In terms of literary communication, negativity is essential as "an enabling structure." But it is a structure or a frame that is unformulated and must be "built up into a coherent whole by the reader's process of ideation."[16] In the formulation of the cause underlying the questioning of the world in the text, the reader must transcend that world. The reader's formulation of negativity enables him or her to observe the world from outside. In Iser's opinion, the true communicatory function of literature lies in this activity. Iser's "negativity" is another way of understanding Ingarden's "core" or "idea," an associative relationship on a level that allows the comprehension of the entire literary work.

The structuralist approach familiar to most readers has conventionally bracketed the object of analysis in such a way as to ignore methodologically factors beyond the level of analysis being carried out. As observed above, however, an inclusive structuralist approach will give attention to the relationship between different levels of structure—extending to the "idea" or "core" or "deeper sense" of life and existence (Ingarden) and the negativity that transcends the particular literary work (Iser).

The Structuralist Tradition and the Hermeneutic Tradition

A real analogy exists between the meaning in the case of a sentence and the meaning of entities that go beyond the sentence, meaning extending to life itself.[17] It is from the meaning or reference of individual words that understanding of the sentence takes place. But there is a reciprocal relationship between the sentence and the word. The various possibilities of word meanings make the meaning of the sentence indeterminate. In the larger processes of life and living, meaning or significance is the result of the relationship between the meaning or reference of the parts and the whole. The various manifestations refer to something that belongs to life, but what is sought is life itself, which does not mean something else.

Both the hermeneutic approach to meaning and the inclusive structuralist approach may be appreciated more fully by giving attention to contemporary mathematical and scientific theories that oppose the sort of scientific approach that employs a linear model of inductive understanding. The work of Alfred Tarski makes clear that any particular system in itself is incomplete (or inconsistent). When the question of verifiable truth is at stake, objects to which a particular sentence refers cannot include the sentence itself. In order to talk about this language, therefore, another language is needed. The language talked about would be the "object language," and the language used for talking about the object language would be the "meta-language." We must recognize that the meta-language of one level becomes the object language of a higher level.

The nature of truth implied in Tarski's conclusions is remarkably similar to the conclusions of hermeneutics.

> It should be noticed that these terms "object-language" and "meta-language" have only a relative sense. If, for instance, we become interested in the notion of truth applying to sentences, not of our original object-language, but of its meta-language, the latter becomes automatically the object-language of our discussion; and in order to define truth for this language, we have to go to a new meta-language—so to speak, to a meta-language of a higher level. In this way we arrive at a whole hierarchy of languages.[18]

The total hierarchy of languages that would be necessary to define the total hierarchy of truths can never be reached. The alternatives, then, are objectivity and incompleteness (moving beyond one system but never arriving at the ultimate system) or completeness and inconsistency (remaining in one system). If a system (a text, a group of texts, or an entire discipline) claims to include itself, it is open to self-contradicton (since the system provides its own exception). On the other hand, if a system excludes itself from what it studies, it is incomplete.

French Structuralism has handled the incompleteness/inconsistency problem by remaining in one system and by ignoring methodologically the relationship of other systems to the literary system under consideration. Earlier structuralists, however, maintained the structuralist conceptualization by incorporating historical and cultural systems and eventually by relating individual readers to the literary and cultural systems. A hermeneutic literary criticism will benefit from the more comprehensive structuralist conceptualization.

The Unity of a Literary Work of Art: New Criticism

The beginning point of the contemporary recontextualizing of biblical writings may be seen as the emphasis on the literary work as a unity to be understood essentially in terms of that literary structure instead of in terms of ideological, historical, or cultural facts. In literary studies in America, this emphasis resulted from New Criticism, which desired to "explain the work by considering it in isolation, as an autonomous whole, whose significance and value are determined without any reference beyond itself."[19]

When the New Critical perspective is applied to biblical literature, the biblical text is interpreted as a structural unity, with each part seen as integral to the whole and as modifying the meaning of the whole. Interpretation, then, involves bringing all parts of the text into a meaningful relationship to the entire text. Whenever possible, one unit in the text is seen as standing in a metaphoric relation to other units and to the total work. A study of the historical books of the Bible from a literary perspective, therefore, would not begin by dissecting each of them into different historical sources but would begin by considering them as unities, as if each were written by one author. Each part of the text would be studied in relation not to the historical setting and activity of the author as editor, but on its own and in relation to other parts. From such a perspective, the meaning of the Joseph story in the book of Genesis

depends as much on its relationship with the Abraham and Isaac stories (Gen.12-36), the primeval history (Gen. 1-11 and Tamar's outwitting of Judah (Gen. 38) as it does on its own internal structure and language. To understand the Joseph story as a microcosm mirroring by its form and content the macrocosm not only of the book of Genesis but also of the entire Bible is the goal of literary interpretation.[20]

Literary criticism from the perspective of New Criticism is analogous to language in which words have meaning as they join with other words. *Synthesis,* rather than *analysis,* is emphasized.

> Because of its insistence that works of literature are wholes whose parts stand in metaphoric relation to one another, literary criticism, conceived of as a language is more agglutinative than analytic. Along the way it may analyze, dissect, distinguish, but its final aim is always assimilative, inclusive. Use of this language, therefore, highlights tensions within texts, because inevitably many of the parts it wants to piece together will not mesh: they may be made up of dissimilar materials, or have non-interlocking gears, or loose ends. . . . Such tensions make the structure of literary works complex and ambiguous, giving their verbal texture richness and density.[21]

To facilitate the achievement of the goal of assimilation of the various parts of a text, New Critics focus on linguistic and literary strategies and structures, such as paradox, shifts, tone, use of wit and subtlety, and particularly the use of irony. Biblical scholars who recapitulate the activity of the New Critics are discovering such strategies and structures in biblical texts. In particular, they are finding the possibility for irony endless. In the study of Genesis, for example, the perspective of irony opens up numerous possibilities in a story such as the sacrifice of Isaac (Genesis 22), as that story is set within the different contexts of the Abraham stories, the totality of the book of Genesis, the entire Pentateuch, the Hebrew scriptures, and then the Hebrew and Christian scriptures as a whole. Irony in the Gospel of Mark may replace the "messianic secret" as the explanation not only for particular episodes but also for the entire framework of the Gospel.

In the beginnings of New Criticism, the assumption was made that the structures immanent in the text could be discovered in abstraction from the author, from the reader, and from the relationships of the text to the world. Biblical study's adoption of New Criticism was accompanied by a reaction to historical and biographical reduction of a text. In recent years, New Critics have stressed that the emphasis of New Criticism on the literary work of art as a "verbal structure of a certain coherence and wholeness" did not and could not be conceived to mean "a denial of the relevance of historical information for the business of poetic interpretation."[22] The following section is directed to the linguistic and literary system and to cultural and individual codes and sets that complete that system.

Codes

Linguistic and Literary Codes

Readers are able to make sense of the words and sentences in a text to the extent that they have mastered the conventions or rules of the language of that text. Knowledge of meanings of words (lexicon) and grammatical and syntactical regulations (codes) that govern a given language in fact enables a reader to determine what a sentence or a simple short text is *saying*. Texts that carry out only a simple referential function may be mastered with such linguistic knowledge and knowledge of the persons, events, ideas, and so on of the real world to which the text is referring. The meaning and significance of literary texts, however, depend on *dynamic* literary codes that coexist with codes of the natural language. The code of the natural language must be coordinated with higher-order literary codes.

Poetry must be interpreted as a higher-order literary code in relation to prose. Special notice has been given by scholars to biblical poetry for many years. The major emphasis has been on the use of a parallelism in poetry that is comparable to rhythm. In rhythm, a series of words or sounds is given, and the reader expects another series to follow, which more or less corresponds to the original series. In classical and most popular poetry, the units are sounds. The poet considers the length of syllables, the stress on them, and related matters. In biblical poetry, the unit is not a sound but an idea. The poet makes a statement that arouses an expectation. To meet the expectation, the poet goes back to the beginning and says the same thing or follows a line of thought parallel to that already laid down.[23] Biblical poetry clearly constitutes a literary code that depends on but is not the same as the code of the biblical languages.

The Bible is full of creative and imaginative bendings and shapings of literal or "normal" language, such as simile and metaphor, image and symbol, apostrophe and personification, and paradox and hyperbole. This creative, or poetic, language is not to be seen simply as a facade for literal language and meaning but as the vehicle for new meanings. These new meanings depend on the meanings conveyed by the natural languages, but they are not the same as those meanings.

Conventions for narrative do not come directly from the natural language. In narrative, the plot is as important as parallelism is for poetry. Plots are arrangements of events into a beginning, a middle, and an end, which together form a completed whole. The events in the plot move toward the resolution of some conflict, and plots are often characterized by the sort of conflict (physical, character, and moral and spiritual) that is resolved in the story. Ingredients of stories are characters (even when the conflict is not essentially between characters), settings, and the strategies for moving the story along in an interesting way and involving the reader in the story.

Narratives exist as smaller units ("forms" or microstructures) within larger literary works—such units as historical account, saga, myth, fairy tale, fable, parable, miracle story, pronouncement story, and instructive narrative. Biblical scholars have long seen the necessity of viewing these smaller units in the light of their literary structure. But the same principles are at work in the larger narrative works (macrostructures). The "historical" books at the beginning of the Old and New Testaments (Genesis through Ezra-Nehemiah—with the exception of Ruth—in the Old Testament and the Gospels and the Acts of the Apostles in the New Testament) are obviously narrative compositions. The stories of Ruth and Jonah and the apocalypses Daniel and Revelation are also to be read in the light of narrative principles.

Discourse material is found as microstructure and macrostructure. Microstructures of discourse include such forms as homily, admonition, confession, illustrative saying, prophetic utterance, juridical saying, wise saying, proverb, riddle, speech, contract, prayer, and song. These types of units are to be found not only within discursive macrostructures, such as the prophetic and epistolary materials of the Bible, but also within narrative macrostructures.

Readers are confronted simultaneously by the multiple levels of the linguistic and literary structures of the writing being read, and they must apply multiple codes. In the case of letters, for example, readers must keep in mind the first-century letter form and the form of the smaller units (the "hymn," for example) used within the letter. In addition, the systematic ordering on the basis of content must be considered. Since appeal is being made to the reader's will as well as to his or her intellect, rhetorical structures (not necessarily ordered by, but not unrelated to, ancient rules of rhetoric) coexist with structures related to subject matter and the different levels of literary genre.

A reader sees a literary text as the result of codes of the natural language plus the codes of a multiplicity of literary languages that supplement the natural language. Two approaches must be taken by the reader simultaneously: the utilization and appreciation of the materials and processes of the subordinate levels, beginning with the natural language; and the formulation, utilization, and appreciation of more and more comprehensive organizations of meaning. Lotman speaks of the "application of a code or a small number of logically connected codes to the message" as a result of the desire for intellectual pleasure.[24] Application of the codes of the Greek language and the letter form might satisfy the desire for intellectual pleasure in the reading of a New Testament letter, for example. Attention to sensuous pleasure must *accompany* the concern for intellectual pleasure for fullest appreciation of biblical literature. Concern for sensuous pleasure "entails the multiple application of diverse codes" and "strives for protraction."[25] When rhetorical and figurative codes supplement those of the letter form and the Greek language, the reading of a letter involves a more sensuous pleasure.

The analogy of the process of digestion of food is used to illustrate the process of sense perception.

> Let us take as a text . . . a piece of food we are eating. The whole process of digestion can be divided into stages of interaction between nerve receptors, acids and enzymes. On every level some portion of what was not assimilated on the previous level, that is, which did not carry information, which was extra-systemic and neutral, joins in the active process of metabolism, becomes systemic and yields the information contained within itself.[26]

Extrinsic and Intrinsic Codes in Literary Criticism

The function of a text is related to the sort of thing the text is taken to "refer" to, to "mean," or to "signify." The function and reference govern the type of codes and strategies to be used and, hence, the structures to be perceived. (The availability of strategies can influence the frame used by the reader, of course.) Austin Warren suggests a nature and function that leads to concentration on the linguistic and literary codes themselves. The "prime and chief function" of literature, according to Warren, is "fidelity to its own nature." The delight of literature, and not its use, is emphasized. This nature and function is felt by "proper" and "instinctive" readers as well as by writers. From the

Romantic movement on, this proper function has been emphasized, with the poet moving away from the equation of the function with extrinsic relations. Whatever usefulness literature has must be subsumed under the major purpose of pleasure. "The pleasure of literature . . . is not one preference among a long list of possible pleasures but is a 'higher pleasure' because pleasure in a higher kind of activity, i.e., non-acquisitive contemplation." The usefulness of literature, then, is consistent with nonacquisitive contemplation. It is a "pleasurable seriousness," an "aesthetic seriousness," a "seriousness of perception."[27]

The extreme view of imminence was stated by an early formalist so as to exclude concern with extrinsic relations: "I am concerned in the theory of literature only with the examination of its inner laws. To use an industrial metaphor, when studying the art of weaving, I am not interested in the situation of the world cotton market, nor in the policy of the cotton trusts, but only in the count of yarn and the techniques of weaving."[28] A colleague countered that the cotton market could not be entirely ignored since the needs of the market have some relation to the development of the technique of weaving. The same is to be said for literature. The linguistic and literary system of a work of art has relevance to the larger society in a complex and dialectical way.

A dialectical relationship exists between intrinsic and extrinsic systems and codes, to be sure, and the New Critical and formalist program requires consideration of extrinsic codes. Nevertheless the severe emphasis on intrinsic study was a dramatic and rhetorical way of denying that the proper role of criticism was to discern the enabling conditions of a literary text. This rhetoric may be helpful in the study of the Bible, for—as with earlier literary study—biblical study has often been equated with the study of the enabling conditions. The linguist who wants to know what the language system (phonology, grammar, semantics) underlying the Bible is like can have his or her intellectual curiosity satisfied. Likewise, the historian who is interested in what happened in the history of Israel and the early church, and the theologian who dreams of a complete picture of the religion of Israel and the early Christian community must use the Bible as a resource. The geneticist has methods of study that give attention to the origins and features of the traditions and documents that made their way into the Bible, the movement from oral to written transmission, the identity of the writers and/or schools involved, the editorial processes, the modification by means of interpolation, scribal errors, and so on. All of these are illustrations of source oriented inquiry. Interest focuses on an object behind the text—the state of affairs or processes of development that operated at the time as a source of biblical writing.[29]

The source oriented extrinsic approaches suggested above are among those standing in opposition to "intrinsic" approaches emphasized with New Criticism. Biblical writings necessarily reflect the material and enabling sources and conditions of their origin. But such approaches by-pass genuine criticism. The text in such cases is seen as the shell with the real meat being the linguistic, historical, and theological information. Once the information is obtained, the shell can be discarded.

Biblical texts and literary texts are being reconceived today in a fashion that emphasizes both the text and the enabling conditions. This has resulted in part because of the impossibility of considering the text in isolation. Conventional and structuralist literary criticism have reincorporated earlier concerns as they have been influenced by speech-act theory, which sees the text as a series of speech acts. Communication has been seen as involving not only acts that have meaning (locutionary acts) but also acts that have a certain force in saying something (illocutionary acts) and acts that achieve certain ends by saying something (perlocutionary acts). Questions of the cultural context are vital. Questions of the author's motivation, sincerity, and strategy and the heuristics of interpretation have come to be emphasized. The progressive enlargement and extension of the New Critical and structural models does not mean that scholars have abandoned the goal of logically consistent analysis and interpretation. What S. R. Levin says of structuralist literary analysis is also true in certain respects of New Criticism, that "the text itself . . . continues to be considered for its internal structure," even though "the relations found to pertain therein are no longer regarded as self-sufficient; they are seen rather, as intentional projections of the author, interpreted constructs of the reader, and semantic mappings onto possible worlds."[30]

Discourse oriented analysis of biblical texts benefits from New Critical and structuralist approaches, but it does not disdain information gained from the original historical context. Such analysis

> sets out to understand not the realities behind the text but the text itself as a pattern of meaning and effect. What does this piece of language—metaphor, epigram, dialogue, tale, cycle, book—signify in context? What are the rules governing the transaction between storyteller or poet and reader? Are the operative rules, for instance, those of prose or verse, parable or chronicle, omniscience or realistic limitation, historical or fictional writing? What image of a world does the narrative project? Why does it unfold the action in this particular order and from this particular viewpoint? What is the part played by the omissions, redundancies, ambiguities, alternations between scene and summary or elevated and colloquial language? How does the work hang together? And, in general in what relationship does part stand to whole and form to function? (*PBN*, p. 15)

Discourse oriented analysis is a productive way of coordinating New Critical and socio-historical emphases. Discourse oriented analysis is an advance on source oriented analysis in that the text is the focus instead of some realities behind the text. Redaction criticism in biblical studies developed into a type of discourse oriented study. The Gospels, for example, came to be seen in the light of their structure and function *vis à vis* their communities. Rhetorical analysis of biblical writings is also a type of discourse oriented approach. For the most part, however, the thrust remains "determinate and stable" and moored in the past. Socio-cultural codes are assumed as constraints upon original speakers/writers and hearers/readers. The discourse is examined as goal-directed activity of a speaker, which requires interpretation by the hearer. The discourse is the center of attention because it embodies the intention of the speaker and guides the response of the hearer.

Cultural Norms and the Reader

The reader-oriented literary approach places the past oriented source and discourse analysis within a literary framework with concern for contemporary meaning for the reader. Intellectual pleasure is not only placed at the disposal of sensuous pleasure but also past meaning is related to present meaning. The reader-oriented approach adopts the hermeneutic tradition, which emphasizes that the process of historical understanding involves past and present traditions. The past is not seen as a closed circle.

> Historical understanding is the endeavor to bring about a meaningful agreement, an agreement in substance, between two traditions, one past, the other present. This whole, therefore, is emphatically not the wholeness of the past tradition in itself. The whole that is projected is not the autonomy of an object that is to stand over against the interpreting subject, for that would be at the outset both to defeat the purpose of understanding, which is the unification of the two parties; and to deny that what is being said concerns the interpreter too. The past is not understood as a closed circle in the sense of a thing in itself that could be understood intrinsically. It is understood only in relation, for understanding it means reaching an understanding between the past and the present.[31]

The hermeneutic circle is not simply the relationship between the parts and the whole of a text. It is the relationship between the text and the expanding contexts within which the text makes sense and involves the historical experience of the reader's understanding of the text or agreeing with the text. The structuralist conceptualization emphasizing the dialectical and complex relationship between intrinsic and extrinsic systems and codes allows us to see how the past and present are related in reading and interpretation in a way to keep the reading process open. The "scientific" linear model of inductive understanding is avoided, as is a totalizing hermeneutic model of understanding. The perspective of life from which all subordinate expressions are to be understood can only be reached in dynamic historical experience.

In early structuralists' experience with literary interpretation, they were discovering what scholars in the hermeneutic and scientific traditions have also discovered: the impossibility of an approach in which neither historicity nor individual valuation plays a part.

Cultural Norms. Different structures result from different perspectives of literary works, and these different perspectives result in part from changes in the extra-literary and literary systems that influence the reading and actualization of literary works.

The influence of culture in determining perspectives and the structuring within each of the different perspectives was stressed in the early structuralist movement. Since extra-literary realities are related to the literary text, the literary text is altered perceptively by changes in extra-literary systems.

Moreover, changes in the literary tradition itself cause changes in the structures perceived in a literary work.

The work of art itself is not a constant. As we shift in time, our social surroundings alters the existing artistic tradition through whose prism the art work is observed, and as a result of such shifts that aesthetic object also changes which in the awareness of a member of a particular collective corresponds to a material artifact—an artistic product.[32]

One way of noting the effect of historical changes on the literary work is to distinguish between the material work of art (work-thing) and the aesthetic object (concretization) that is actualized on the basis of the material work. Instead of seeing the difference between the work and its changing actualizations as something negative (a result of the incompleteness of artistic creativity or of perception), early structuralists came to see the changes as belonging "to the very basis of aesthetic value, which is a process and not a state, *energeia* and not *ergon*."[33]

In biblical studies, the distinction between the material work itself and what the work comes to be in the perception and actualization of readers has been taken to be the result of a lack of information and/or critical capacity. As knowledge and capacity develop, more accurate perception and actualization take place. But it seems impossible to dispute the idea that biblical texts have been perceived differently because of different world views and because of developments within a particular world view. The ancient and medieval church could only perceive the Bible in the light of its Platonic world view, and the church following the Enlightenment could not perceive the Bible apart from consideration of its historicity. Changes in perception within the historical paradigm are obvious to students of the Bible. The movement from source, to form, to redaction, and composition criticism may be seen as the failure of textual data to be saturated by one particular insight and approach. The data that were not saturated became the basis for a new perspective. In the process, then, there is a movement to the center of interest of elements that had been ignored or at the periphery in earlier approaches. Even with the same general historical moment and approach, differences are possible. In redaction criticism, radically different historical and theological contexts may be postulated and supported with the same textual data. Different perceptions of the context, in fact, result in different perceptions of the literary relationships within biblical texts and in different meanings.

The influence of changes in culture on perception of biblical data may be illustrated from Krister Stendahl's view of the church's treatment of Paul's concept of the law in Romans. Stendahl points out that Paul's writings meant relatively little for the thinking of the church during the first 350 years of its history. It is with Augustine that Paul becomes important. A decisive reason for this state of affairs, according to Stendahl, is that up to the time of Augustine the church saw Paul as dealing with issues that were not relevant to the church. These issues are: What happens to the actual Law of Moses when the Messiah has come? What does the Messiah's arrival mean for the relationship between

Jews and Gentiles? These were not live issues after the end of the first century, for the constituency of Christianity was essentially non-Jewish. With Augustine, Paul's thought on the law and justification was applied consistently to the problem of a plagued conscience. With Augustine, then, Paul begins to be interpreted not in the light of a Pauline characteristic but in the light of the Western characteristic of an "introspective conscience." Stendahl is insistent that Augustine's move is inconsistent with the intention of Paul, for "we look in vain for any evidence that *Paul the Christian* had suffered under the burden of conscience concerning personal shortcomings which he would label 'sins.' "[34]

Luther's interpretation of Paul, according to Stendahl, maintained and intensified the problem of conscience because his interpretation was colored by developments in late medieval piety and theology, in particular the developed system of penance and indulgences. "When the period of the European mission had come to an end, the theological and practical center of Penance shifted from Baptism, administered once and for all, to the ever repeated Mass, and already this subtle change in the architecture of the Christian life contributed to a more acute introspection." Luther "carries out his mission as a great pioneer" in response to the question of the Christians who took seriously the practice of self-examination: "How can I find a gracious God?" In that context, "Paul's words about a justification in Christ by faith, and without the works of the Law, appear as the liberating and saving answer."[35]

Ernst Käsemann's strenuous criticism of Stendahl's thesis points out the influence of the different historical situations of Stendahl and Käsemann on the way they read Paul's work. Käsemann contrasts his own Reformation approach and the "salvation history" approach of Stendahl. In the tradition of Stendahl, the scriptural theology of the Reformation tradition "has been pushed aside . . . by a theology which is guided by the needs of the church or its traditions." The exposition of the Bible "is regulated and confined by considerations of edification or by the self-understanding which is prevailing at any given moment." Stendahl's interpretation of the Bible as salvation history "allows us to think in terms of a development which, in spite of many false starts and many needful corrections, leads to growing understanding and ultimately to the goal which the church has before it, a goal whose outline is already to be traced in the church itself." Käsemann is opposed to the practical result of the church's taking precedence over the scriptures—"even when this is not admitted in principle or is dialectically obscured."

> In no case should what we call the divine plan of salvation be absorbed by an immanent evolutionary process whose meaning can be grasped on earth, or which we can control and calculate. This would make the divine and the human interchangeable and would allow the church ultimately to triumph over its Lord, by organizing him instead of listening and obeying.[36]

It might be thought that we have here a defense of an interpretation that is capable of ignoring its own context. However, Käsemann reveals his own "systematic prejudice" and cultural containment in his acknowledgment that salvation history, for him, is tied up with the Third Reich.

> My theological youth was most strongly marked by the detachment of 'dialectical' theology from the nineteenth-century idealist view of history. . . . On the way to a theology of proclamation we rediscovered that Reformation doctrine of justification which had become largely incomprehensible to our fathers and grandfathers and which had therefore ceased for them to form the centre of the New Testament message. This discovery immunized us deeply against a conception of salvation history which broke in on us in secularized and political form with the Third Reich and its ideology. It will be understandable that as burnt children we are unwilling to add fuel to the fire which at the present day, for the third time in a century is awaking such general enthusiasm. Our experience has made a theology of history suspect for us from the very outset, whatever the reasons may be which are urged in its support. It determined the liberalism whose faith in progress was finally shattered by the First World War. However erroneously and improperly, it was capable of serving as a shield for Nazi eschatology. We do not want to be called back to the place where our fathers and grandfathers stood a hundred years ago and where they came to grief fifty years later.[37]

Biblical texts are perceived and interpreted in quite different ways as a result of changes in world view and in social surroundings within any given world view. These changes alter the tradition through whose prism the text is observed. The changes in perception of biblical texts, then, do not necessarily mean that scholars have moved closer to the true nature of the biblical text. Changes in the structures result from different world views and from different perceptions.

It is clear that for Augustine and Luther, for Stendahl and Käsemann, and for individuals and groups with different approaches in different epochs the same thing has been done. Readers have been reducing the text to their idiom, naturalizing the text so that it speaks to them. Even the most radical scientific approach that intends to avoid the error of "modernizing" the text may be seen as a way of naturalizing the text—when the reader's context is a positivistic scientism. How else could the text make sense for such a reader?

A reader-oriented approach acknowledges that the contemporary reader's "intending" of the text is not the same as that of the ancient author and/or the ancient readers. This is not possible, necessary, or desirable. The fact that the text is biblical does not change the picture, for the contemporary reader will no more find the pristine meaning and significance of the author in the biblical text than in any artistic text. But is there not continuity between the past and the present? Is it not possible that the reader's "intention" is of a piece with the author's intention and with the meaning and significance found by earlier readers with different views? This will mean not that there is no meaning, but that meanings discovered in different epochs are authentic—that meaning discovered with approaches that are informed by discourse and hermeneutic oriented insights are authentic in the same fashion—not final, but satisfying and authentic.

The challenge today is that our world view does

not dictate one perspective and approach. The Bible may be approached as the means of obtaining or confirming confessional religious truths (corresponding to the dogmatic approach of the ancient and medieval church) and/or as a record of ancient religious belief and practice. It may be approached as a means of contemporary self-understanding and self-renewal and/or a record of those experiences in the ancient peoples of the Bible. It may be approached as the expression of individual and social structures and processes. Even when it is approached as language and literature, different emphases are possible: the biblical languages, the development from early oral and written sources to completed works, the structures and effects of the completed works upon the original recipients, the history of the reception of the works, and/or the meaning and significance for readers today.

The capacity of the contemporary reader to entertain the possibility of alternative approaches and even to embrace various approaches (instead of attempting to establish one exclusive approach) need not be seen as a failure of nerve or a loss of religious or academic faith. The interpenetration of approaches is vital for full appreciation and application of any one approach.[38] The interpenetration of approaches is also necessary to do full justice to the text. The simultaneous functioning of the text as literature and as history and/or theology is necessary for the appreciation of the text as text. Today, scholars are giving attention to aesthetic, emotive, and conative functions of biblical texts, but this turn in the history of interpretation does not deny that biblical texts had particular practical referential functions and that they continue to have practical functions. In fact, in the real life of a culture, texts often *must* perform different functions at the same time in order to be effective.

> Under certain conditions, so that an icon may be perceived as a religious text and perform this social function, it must also be a work of art. The reverse dependence is also possible. In order to be perceived as a work of art, the icon must have the religious function that is proper to it. Therefore, its transfer to a museum (and, in a certain sense, the absence of religious feeling in the viewer) violates the effect, historically inherent to the text, of the unity of the two social functions.[39]

This multifunctional nature is related directly to literature.

> The unification of the artistic function with the magical, juridical, moral, philosophical, and political constitutes an inalienable feature of the social functioning of an artistic text. A bilateral connection is frequently present: so that it may perform a particular belletristic function, a text must simultaneously have moral, political, philosophical, and publicistic functions.[40]

The contemporary context for biblical reading and interpretation allows and encourages different perspectives. In the history of biblical study, certain views of the world and/or strong individuals and schools dictated particular perspectives and approaches that became dominant. Today pluralism reigns. When the goal of biblical study is "intellectual pleasure," the determination of the one meaning and significance of a text, the current situation is one of radical disorientation with little hope of reorientation. A reader oriented goal that is directed to a more comprehensive "sensuous pleasure," however, may help to reorient the field. The following section depicts a move from a concern with the role of culture to the role of the individual in reading and interpretation.

The Individual Reader. The roles assigned to the individual and to culture have evolved in the various structuralist epochs, and the dialectical relationship of individual and culture seen by the structuralist tradition is helpful in our contemporary reader-oriented approach. In the early stages, the role of the reader was assumed to be that of the autonomous critic who was able to analyze the structures of the autonomous text in a disinterested way. The historicity of the text and the historicity of the reader were ignored.

When the structuralists first moved beyond concern with the intrinsic organization of linguistic and literary elements to include cultural and social factors, the structuralist conceptualization was maintained by viewing the literary system as a part of and interacting with cultural and social systems. The reader was seen only as a passive vehicle of the supra-individual structures. Individual aesthetic judgment reflected "the collective nature and character of aesthetic evaluation." Evidence for the existence and control of this collective is the fact that "for the evaluator, situated in a specific time and place, and in a given social milieu, any particular value of some work appears to him as necessary and constant."[41]

The role of a given culture in determining the

perspective of individual readers cannot be denied. In the period of ascendancy of the historical and existential approaches in biblical studies, for example, individual readers undoubtedly viewed the reigning approach and its value as "necessary and constant." Certainly this was true for the dogmatic approach of the ancient and medieval church. In our epoch, no one approach and value has such power. The individual reader and groups of readers and their involvement in the creation of meaning have become central today.

This was the focus of a stage of early structuralist activity, and the insights of that period remain pertinent. In the 1940s, Mukarovsky moved beyond cultural codes and saw the individual subject as an active force necessary for the genesis of meaning. In his lecture on "Intentionality and Unintentionality In Art" (1943), Mukarovsky sees that in works of art it is intentionality "which binds together the individual parts and components of a work into the unity that gives the work its meaning." This intentionality is not the aim or purpose to be achieved by means of the works; it is the attitude of the perceiver. During the perception of a work of art, the perceiver takes an attitude toward the object and immediately attempts to find in the organization of the work evidence of an arrangement that allows the work to be seen as a semantic whole.[42] When the structures and functions of a work are looked at from the point of view of an individual, they appear "as a set of live energies which are in constant tension and conflict with one another."[43] In the process of perception, new signs are perceived on the basis of previously determined perceptions and meanings, and the new signs that are apprehended change to a greater or lesser extent the meaning of everything that has preceded.

Does the reader's activity go beyond determination of the individual literary work? When the reader is seen as an integral component of the creation of the aesthetic object, and extra-literary systems are seen as integrally related to the literary system, the reader *must* also be seen as related to the actualization of extra-literary systems. Actualization has to do with factors in the linguistic-literary system such as the "author," literary categories such as genre, literary epochs, the literature of an entire nation, and literature as a whole.[44] But it also has to do with factors in systems impinging upon the linguistic-literary system. A dynamic relationship exists among all of these factors.

The importance of the reader has not been totally ignored in literary studies, but the contribution of the individual reader has been seen as interfering with literature and as a variable to be discounted. Recent psychological studies, however, have enabled us to envision the contribution of individual readers in a fashion whereby the individual contribution is not purely idiosyncratic. Cognitive psychology and psychoanalytically oriented literary studies help us to see how readers' perceptions depend on the stages of development and/or the psychological "set" of the readers. Different individuals (and even the same individual at different stages of development) will perceive or actualize the same literary object differently.

Consideration of the influence of a dynamically evolving subject in literary hermeneutics goes back at least to Wilhelm Dilthey's dissatisfaction with the idea of a transcendental-subjective, apriori, ahistorical, asocial, and acultural pure reason. Dilthey's interest in the subject grew out of the impossibility of discovering a final objective ground for knowledge. A virtue was made of this impossibility by envisioning the subject in terms of a system that unites all factors as variables in such a way that "the dynamic totality of this unification forms an open, self-controlling, and self-correcting system, in short, a 'learning' system."[45]

Contemporary structural psychology denies that humans are merely passive reactors to the environment or, on the other hand, possessors of "innate ideas" that automatically unfold. The stages of development deduced from Jean Piaget's study of children (the sensorimotor stage, the stage of concrete operations, and the stage of formal operations) have been applied by various scholars to the development of an individual's concern with the otherness of people, ideas, and ideals and to development in the individual's symbolic capacity.

With the help of the Piagetian conceptualization, we may view the development of interpretative competence in terms of stages (using the concept of interpretation as the discernment of linguistic and literary structure by means of codes). An advanced stage would be the reader's generation of new meanings by means of the potential of the text, offered by the codes and structures of the natural language and the supplementary literary codes and structures. This is comparable to the antifoundationalist view of knowledge as the result of interdependent systems, which include experience and life. The most basic stage, of course, would be the reduction of the structures and meanings to those made possible by application of the grammar and syntax of the natural language. Intermediate stages would give attention to a limited number of codes and would limit structures and meanings to those authenticated by the culture of the reader and/or to only one level of meaning.

Lotman's analogy of the chemical analysis of sea water may help us to distinguish not only between different conceptualizations of the structure of the artistic text (Lotman's concern) but also between stages of development of the perceiving subject. The conceptualization of the text as conveying constant information may be compared to the reasoning of the scientist who sees in sea water a particular case of water in general. When the formula H_2O has been separated, the analysis is complete for the scientist, and the remainder of the composition is taken to be "outside the system." The view of the text as an addition of static codes corresponds to a second stage, when the scientist discovers the presence of a number of other ingredients in sea water. By setting out the different chemical formulas of these additional ingredients, the scientist acknowledges the mixture of different substances to be a fact. A third view of the text is advocated by Lotman, one comparable to a third stage, when sea water acquires for the researcher "the character of an integral chemical mechanism with its own structure and internal self-regulation combining a unity of dynamic and static principals, a mechanism manifesting qualities and potentialities which would not be characteristic of any other separate components or parts."[46]

Understanding and acceptance of some progression in the symbolic capacity of readers does not contribute directly to development of a method of literary interpretation. Nevertheless it may serve to relativize the interpretation of a particular reader, to encourage a reader to acknowledge the possibility of other and different readings without necessarily invalidating the particular reader's interpretation.

Insight into the influence of the reader's own psychological "set" in literary interpretation grows out of psychoanalytic oriented studies. In an early stage, the text was seen as the expression of the experiences of the author.[47] A central fantasy of the author has been transformed into social, moral, and intellectual terms in the literary text. These fantasies are defined according to customary phases of the child's development, distinguished by parts of the body or family that provide most pleasure or conflict for the child at the time. The literary text is not, however, simply the writer's disguised expression of childhood fantasies. The fantasies have been defended against, and it is only in an oblique way that they are expressed. Because of this dual nature of the text, it may be seen from the dimension of the expression (social, intellectual, moral, and religious concerns of the text) or it may be seen as that which is expressed (the dark, chthonic, primitive, bodily part of mental life). The social, moral, and intellectual expressions in the text must be analyzed to discern the central fantasy, or daydream, that has been transformed into that particular content.

Later psychoanalytic-oriented work emphasizes the reader; a reader's response to a literary text is determined by the reader's own life-style.[48] The psychoanalytic grounding is evident in that the life-style of the reader is defined in terms of past events, which create an "identity theme." This identity theme is seen as established in the first stage of a child's development, even though it grows through experiences (which can be seen as new variations) into a more fixed central theme. The reader's "identity theme" has to do with the particular style of defense and adaptation and in terms of wish-fulfilling fantasies.

The principal of defense is important in the reader centered stage of study because a reader's favorable response to a work indicates that the reader has found in the work something related to what he or she does to cope with needs or dangers. (Defense mechanisms are seen not as pathological and undesirable blocks to normal pleasure, but as "necessary adaptations to inner and outer reality, preconditions without which pleasure would not be possible.")[49]

The principal of fantasy is involved because readers use materials taken in from the literary work to create the wish-fulfilling fantasy characteristic of themselves. The synthesis of the defense structures is "both tricky and subtle," but the use of the story to get the desired fantasy content is "no trouble at all." "The ego's defenses act like a doorkeeper carefully checking invitations against the list of acceptable guests. Once the guests are admitted, however, the party turns out to be not stuffy at all, but quite easy going, even a bit rowdy and disreputable."[50]

Once the reader has matched personal defense structures and adapted these to suit individual fantasies, the reader will "make sense" of the text. That is, the reader will transform the fantasy content into some literary point or theme of interpretation. In this experience, the reader uses "higher" ego functions, such as interpretive skills, literary experience, and experience of human character. The social, moral, or political ideas that already embody congenial transformations for the reader are brought to bear. The fantasy will be synthesized as an intellectual content that is characteristic and pleasing for the reader.

The view of the text as consisting of both static and dynamic structures, structures that constitute a potentiality for the reader's critical and creative activities, is congenial to the view psychology takes of the activity of the reader. The literary work offers constraints for the work of the reader, but the reader makes a distinctive contribution. The reader "shapes as he perceives, splitting into parts, adding to and omitting from, until his perception matches his particular and adaptive structures."[51]

It is not necessary to accept the details of psychoanalytic explanations of an individual's "set" to find value in the emphasis on the influence of individuality in the process of reading. Barbara Herrnstein Smith finds such a reality at work in her reading of Shakespeare. "Sonnets that I had never assigned to a class and disdained to comment upon will, during a half-casual re-reading, suddenly leap from the page and startle me into awe and recognition—often because, since last reading it, I have lived the poem, lived something like its occasion or something like its motive."[52] Her explanation of this phenomenon utilizes the idea of a psychological "set."

> Our interpretation of a work and our experience of its value are mutually dependent, and each depends upon what might be called the psychological "set" of our encounter with it: not the "setting" of the work, or, in the narrow sense, its context, but rather the nature and potency of our own assumptions, expectations, capacities and interests with respect to it—our "prejudices" if you like, but hardly to be distinguished from our identity (or *who*, in fact, *we are*) at the time of the encounter. Moreover, all three—the interpretation, the evaluation, and the "set"—operate and interact in the same fashion as the hermeneutic circle itself: that is, simultaneously causing and justifying themselves and causing and justifying each other.[53]

Readers *make* sense. Readers may perform their role constrained by their cultural contexts and critical assumptions and remain unaware of their potential as creative readers. When readers become conscious of their role, the process of reading is altered. Readers regain their own voices. They may revel in the freedom and potential offered by particular texts, but a share of the freedom of textual interpretation results from the fact that readers are no longer constrained by traditional dogmatic and/or historical-critical goals of reading and interpretation. Readers play a role in the conception of functions of biblical texts that match their experiences and needs. Chapter 4 deals with the conception of the role and function of scripture and the sacred in a postmodern epoch, and Chapter 5 concerns the basic strategies in reading and interpretation of texts.

Notes

1. Ferdinand de Saussure, *Course in General Linguistics*, rev. ed., eds. Charles Bally and Albert Sechehaye in collaboration with Albert Riedlinger, trans. Wade Baskin (London: Peter Owen, 1974), p. 123.

2. Ibid.

3. Even though grammatical associative series exist in language as concrete entities and not just as abstract categories, Saussure indicates that "we never know exactly whether or not the awareness of speakers goes as far as the analyses of the grammarians" (ibid., p. 138).

4. Ibid., p. 124.

5. Charles Sanders Peirce, *Collected Papers*, I (Cambridge, Mass.: Harvard University Press, 1931-35), p. 295.

6. Saussure, *Course in General Linguistics*, p. 71. Derrida transfers the differential nature of the signifier and signified to the sign even though the sign for Saussure comes to be a fixed entity for the community. See Jacques Derrida, "Différance," in *Margins of Philosophy*, trans. Alan Bass (Chicago: University of Chicago Press, 1982), pp. 10-11.

7. Umberto Eco, "A Semiotic Approach to Semantics," *Versus* 1 (1971):25.

8. Peirce is directly idealistic in his conception of the relation of the human and the sign. Although "things which are relative to the mind doubtless are," apart from that relation, it is also true that "there is no thing which is in-itself in the sense of not being relative to the mind" (Peirce, *Collected Papers*, V, p. 186). Saussure comes from the other direction in his discussion of the associative relationships. In his discussion of such things as abstract grammatical entities and word order, Saussure indicates that "the important thing is that *abstract entities are*

always based in the last analysis, on concrete entities. No grammatical abstraction is possible without a series of material elements as a basis, and in the end we must always come back to these elements." Although word order is "unquestionable an abstract entity," it exists solely because of "the concrete units that contain it and that flow in a single dimension. To think that there is an incorporeal syntax outside material units distributed in space would be a mistake." In practice, the relations that linguistic terms have outside discourse are a result of association in the memory of language users. "Through its grasp of the nature of the relations that bind the terms together, the mind creates as many associative series as there are diverse relations" (Saussure, *Course in General Linguistics,* pp. 138, 139, 125).

9. Saussure, *Course in General Linguistics,* p. 130

10. Roman Jakobson, "Closing Statement: Linguistics and Poetics," in *Semiotics: An Introductory Anthology,* ed. Robert E. Innis (Bloomington: Indiana University Press, 1985), p. 155.

11. Ibid., pp. 154, 155, 165.

12. See Edgar V. McKnight, *Meaning in Texts: The Historical Shaping of a Narrative Hermeneutics* (Philadelphia: Fortress Press, 1978), pp. 279-85 for a full analysis using Bremond's model.

13. Roman Ingarden, *The Literary Work of Art: An Investigation of the Borderlines of Ontology, Logic, and Theory of Literature,* trans. George G. Grabowicz. Northwestern Studies in Phenomenology and Existential Philosophy (Evanston, Ill.: Northwestern University Press, 1973), pp. 29-30. See McKnight, *The Bible and the Reader,* pp. 26-36.

14. Roman Ingarden, *The Cognition of the Literary Work of Art,* trans. Ruth Ann Crowley and Kenneth R. Olson. Northwestern Studies in Phenomenology and Existential Philosophy (Evanston, Ind.: Northwestern University Press, 1973), p. 85.

15. Wolfgang Iser, *The Act of Reading: A Theory of Aesthetic Response* (London: Routledge & Kegan Paul, 1978), pp. 225, 226, 229.

16. Ibid., p. 225.

17. Wilhelm Dilthey, *Gesammelte Schriften*, VII, 5th ed. (Göttingen: Vandenhoeck & Ruprecht, 1968), pp. 233-34, 240. See McKnight, *Meaning in Texts*, pp. 7-32.

18. Alfred Tarski, "The Semantic Conception of Truth," in *Readings in Philosophical Analysis*, eds. Herbert Feigland and Wilfrid Sellars (New York: Appleton-Century-Crofts, 1949), p. 60. Cited in Joel C. Weinsheimer, *Gadamer's Hermeneutics: A Reading of "Truth and Method"* (New Haven, Conn.: Yale University Press, 1985), pp. 55-56.

19. M. H. Abrams, *The Mirror and the Lamp: Romantic Theory and the Critical Tradition* (New York: W. W. Norton, 1958), p. 7.

20. David Robertson, *The Old Testament and the Literary Critic* (Philadelphia: Fortress Press, 1977), p. 7.

21. Ibid.

22. René Wellek, *Concepts of Criticism*, ed. Stephen G. Nichols, Jr. (New Haven, Conn.: Yale University Press, 1963), p. 7.

23. Robert Lowth, *Lectures on the Sacred Poetry of the Hebrews*, trans. G. Gregory (London: J. Johnson, 1878). Lowth himself distinguished three types of parallelism: synonymous, antithetic, and synthetic. In synonymous parallelism, the thought expressed in the second clause is the same as that in the first. When the thought of the second is in contrast with that of the first, antithetic parallelism results. Climactic parallelism is used to advance the thought, the second clause repeating part of the first clause and also adding additional elements to it. In cases where no specific relationship between clauses can be detected on the basis of content, the term *formal parallelism* is applied.

24. Jurij Lotman, *The Structure of the Artistic Text*, Michigan Slavic Contributions 7, trans. Gail Lenhoff and Ronald Vroon (Ann Arbor: University of Michigan Press, 1977), pp. 58-60.

25. Ibid., pp. 58-59.

26. Ibid., p. 58.

27. Austin Warren, "The Function of Literature," in René Wellek and Austin Warren, *Theory of Literature* (New York: Harcourt, Brace & Co., 1942), pp. 21, 28.

28. Viktor Sklovskij, *O teorii prozy*. See Thomas G. Winner, "The Aesthetics and Poetics of the Prague Linguistic Circle," *Poetics* 8 (1973):80.

29. Meir Sternberg, *The Poetics of Biblical Narrative: Ideological Literature and the Drama of Reading* (Bloomington: Indiana University Press, 1985), p. 15. All excerpts copyright © 1985. Used by permission. Hereafter referred to in the text as *PBN*.

30. Samuel R. Levin, "On the Progress of Structural Poetics," *Poetics* 8 (1979):513-15.

31. Joel C. Weinsheimer, *Gadamer's Hermeneutics: A Reading of "Truth and Method,"* p. 177.

32. Jan Mukarovsky, *Aesthetic Function, Norm and Value as Social Facts* (Ann Arbor: Department of Slavic Languages and Literature, University of Michigan, 1970), pp. 60-61.

33. Ibid., p. 64.

34. Krister Stendhal, "The Apostle Paul and the Introspective Conscience of the West," *Harvard Theological Review* 56 (1963):202-5.

35. Ibid., p. 203.

36. Ernst Käsemann, "Justification and Salvation History in the Epistle to the Romans," in *Perspectives on Paul* (Philadelphia: Fortress Press, 1971), p. 63. All excerpts copyright © 1971. Used by permission.

37. Ibid., pp. 63-64.

38. Sternberg acknowledges that even though "when all is said and done, the independent knowledge we possess of the 'real world' behind the Bible remains absurdly meager," the analysis of a text as discourse may presuppose the reconstruction of various sources—"the Bible's language system, cultural milieu, theology, dating, development within the canon, origins, and transmissional fortunes" (*PBN*, p. 16). The same relationship exists between past-oriented source and discourse approaches and the present-oriented hermeneutic approach.

39. Jurij Lotman, *Analysis of the Poetic Text*, ed. and trans. D. Barton Johnson (Ann Arbor, Mich.: Ardis, 1975), p. 7.

40. Ibid.

41. Mukarovsky, *Aesthetic Function, Norm and Value as Social Facts*, pp. 66, 67, 83.

42. Jan Mukarovsky, "Intentionality and Unintentionality in Art," in *Structure, Sign, and Function: Selected Essays by Jan Mukarovsky*, eds. and trans. John Burbank and Peter Steiner (New Haven, Conn.: Yale University Press, 1978), p. 96.

43. Jan Mukarovsky, "On Structuralism," in *Structure, Sign, and Function: Selected Essays by Jan Mukarovsky*, p. 13.

44. The structure-organization of the author, for example, is not firmly established before interaction with the literary work. It comes into existence through concretization. See Felix Vodicka, "Die Konkretisation des Literarischen Werks: Zur Problematik der Rezeption von Nerudas Werk," in *Die Struktur der Literarischen Entwicklung*, ed. Jurij Striedter (Munich: Wilhelm Fink, 1976), p. 114.

45. Peter Krausser, *Kritik der endlichen Vernunft: Wilhelm Diltheys Revolution der allgemeinen Wissenschafts- und Handlungstheorie* (Frankfurt: Suhrkamp Verlag, 1968), p. 210.

46. Jurij Lotman, "The Future for Structural Poetics," *Poetics* 8 (1979):504.

47. Norman Holland, *The Dynamics of Literary Response* (New York: W. W. Norton, 1968).

48. Norman Holland, *Five Readers Reading* (New Haven, Conn.: Yale University Press, 1975).

49. Ibid., pp. 115-16.

50. Ibid., p. 121.

51. Ibid., p. 247.

52. Barbara Herrnstein Smith, "Fixed Marks and Variable Constancies: A Parable of Literary Value," *Poetics Today* 1 (1979):12. Used by permission of the publisher.

53. Ibid., pp. 16-17.

Chapter Four

The Role of the Reader:

Imaging the Sacred

The Bible assumes the sacred and makes no attempt to accommodate readers who do not share this assumption. The critical approach, on the other hand, *methodologically* ignores the sacred; and critical assumptions and approaches make it difficult to image the sacred. Approaches that see knowledge as necessarily involving life and experience may enable the reimaging of the sacred. This approach is not the same as the critical exegesis of biblical passages that explicate the nature and activity of God.

The Bible as literature shares the assumption of sacrality in such passages, but the Bible as literature discloses the sacred. Indeed, the indirect image of the sacred gained from a literary approach may challenge the explicit teaching concerning the sacred gained from particular passages. The conception of a contemporary literary role for the Bible must be developed, and a view of the unity of the Bible in terms of literature (rather than in terms of dogma or history) must be explicated before the literary imaging of the sacred can be treated. These three interrelated themes are treated in this chapter.

Conceiving a Contemporary Role and Function of the Bible

Are the nature and content of the Bible consistent with a literary orientation? Is the Bible as sacred scripture not compromised by a literary approach? How is a reader-oriented approach to be reconciled with a text-oriented approach? These questions must be faced in conceiving a literary approach to the Bible.

The Bible's Appeal to the Reader and the Literary Nature of the Bible

Biblical texts were composed originally in the Hebrew, Aramaic, and Greek languages, but they were also composed in the secondary languages, or codes, of imaginative literature. Historical and theological references, for example, are embedded in and combined with secondary literary languages, or codes, that speak to readers in a way different from the overt communication of dogmatic or historical writings. As a result, the biblical text is like the artistic text in general, which is so filled with meaning that it "transmits different information to different readers in proportion to each one's comprehension." This ability of the artistic text "to correlate with the reader and provide him with just the information he needs and is prepared to receive" is a notable characteristic of the biblical text.[1]

The rabbis construed Psalm 29:4 as meaning: "The voice of the Lord is in *your* power" by supplying *your* for the possessive pronoun, omitted in the Hebrew text ("his or its power"). The emphasis of the rabbis is on an understanding related to the capacity of each individual hearer. The text is like manna. To the young men it tasted like bread; to the old, honey; to infants, like their mother's milk. But all ate of the manna. The Bible's concern for the reader has been spoken of as "foolproof composition," a strategy whereby the "discourse strives to open and bring home its essentials to all readers so as to establish a common ground, a bond instead of a barrier of understanding" (*PBN*, p. 50).

This characterization of the Bible may be compared to T. S. Eliot's concept of the "magic" of Shakespeare: "For the simplest audience there is the plot, for the more thoughtful the character and the conflict of character, for the more literary the words and phrasing, for the more musically sensitive the rhythm, and for auditors of greater sensitiveness and understanding a meaning which reveals itself gradually."[2]

The literary nature of the Bible is due not to writers' concern with *belles lettres* but to their concern with readers. Meir Sternberg refuses to view the Bible as literature in terms of "art for arts sake" (*PBN*, pp. 35-41). He is convinced that such a view would cause us to lose sight of the historiographic principle regulating biblical narrative. Nevertheless he acknowledges that a reader-oriented aesthetic is a functional principle that must accompany historiography as well as ideology in a study of biblical narrative.[3] "The most comprehensive ground on which ideology and aesthetics meet to shape history" is seen as a strategy related to the reader: "They join forces to originate a strategy of telling that casts reading as a drama, interpretation as an ordeal that enacts and distinguishes the human predicament. It is here that the three regulating principles merge into a single poetics, where their interests and formations so coalesce that they can hardly be told apart in the finished message" (*PBN,* p. 45).[4]

Other writers are less cautious in their view of the Bible as literature. Even the prophets use language in the same fashion as poets, Stephen A. Geller points out, "manipulating its potentialities, consciously or unconsciously, to produce structures rich in meaning and forceful in emotion." Limitation of the poetic work of the prophets to dogmatic purposes is rightly condemned by Geller. "To declare that a poem may not be studied as such violates the principles of science, literature and language."[5]

The biblical writings are designed for readers who will find and create meanings that involve them, that match their needs and capacity at cognitive and non-cognitive levels. This intention has been successful, not only for the particular historical readers, envisioned by the writers, but also for readers implicit in the authors' vision and intention but unknown to the authors. In different epochs, with different world views, the Bible has spoken to different readers.

The dogmatic approach of the ancient and medieval world, the historical approach introduced with the Enlightenment, and the existential approach associated with the name of Rudolf Bultmann have all provided readers with the "information" they needed and were prepared to receive. Earlier referentially or source-oriented approaches, however, were circuitous in this operation. Dogmatic and historical information gleaned from the text was put into dogmatic and/or historical contexts which were meaningful for the reader. From a reader-oriented literary view, this treated the text or the texture like the shell of a nut—the nut was extracted and the shell was discarded. The essence of the text (the nut) in such approaches is its authentic historical data or the logically deduced theological position that clarifies and is clarified by some postulated historical circumstance. To see the Bible as literature, however, is to value both the texture and the content.

Conceiving a Literary Function for Scripture

A comprehensive reader-oriented role and function of biblical literature is capable of mediating and unifying the functions of biblical texts as scripture and as literature. The conventional views of the roles and functions of literature and scripture make mediation problematic. James Kugel says that he has "shuddered to hear it said that Joseph is 'one of the most believable characters in Western literature' " (that is, to subject the biblical text to literary criteria). His objection is that "one wants to say that Joseph is no character at all but someone far more intimately ours."

> That initial literary act, "Come gather round and let me spin a tale," is not quite the starting-point of even this most tale-like part of the Pentateuch. Its premise—"Let me tell you what happened to Joseph-your-ancestor, let me tell you how things came to be as you know them actually to be"—is significantly different. Not to speak of

"Let me tell you how God has saved us," "Let me tell you God's teachings."[6]

The problem of devaluation of biblical texts through a literary approach does not seem to exist today from the literary perspective. Literature views the "tale" as rather profound in its implication for the reader's self-creation or even self-transcendence. The problem may come from the religious perspective. Kugel, for example, seems to feel that viewing the Bible as literature necessarily ignores the religious nature of biblical texts.

> The fact is, at a certain point these tales and songs, prayers and chronicles, began to be stitched together, first figuratively and then literally; *biblia* became a singular noun and, among Christians, came to include both Old and New. This act, or series of acts, changed not only the text but as well the rules of literary competence. For now not only were prophetic oracles and divine legislation invested in holiness, but everything associated with them, sagas, court histories, genealogies, songs, proverbs—all now, through a doctrine of divine inspiration, were associated by common authorship: one Book, one Author, and a special set of rules for reading it in keeping with its unique provenance.[7]

The narrow dogmatic view of the role and function of scripture does preclude the full appreciation of the Bible as literature. As we have seen, however, the dogmatic view of the ancient and medieval church is a historically constrained view and is not the only way to see the function of biblical literature—even in the church. Moreover, the literary criticism that is appropriate for biblical study is one that is open to "foreign elements" from disciplines such as philosophy and theology as well as linguistics, sociology, and psychology. In fact, the literary view advocated in this book supports the possibility of "the ongoing canonization of Scripture," which is called for by Kugel himself.[8]

Although the uniqueness of the Bible is stressed, Kugel suggests that today's literary criticism of the Bible

> can indeed delight us and illuminate the text in surprising ways. Moreover, in seeking to bring together the work of different disciplines and sensibilities, the philologist's and the literary critic's, the Ancient Near Eastern historian's and the moralist's, our own day's criticism may yet perform an act of synthesis comparable in a more profound way to rabbinic writings, an act of *reading* in the contemporary sense, one which will address the complexity of the Bible's present dilemma and so take on the true calling of midrash, viz., the ongoing canonization of Scripture.[9]

A radical reader-oriented view of the role and nature of biblical texts as literature may perform precisely the synthesis that is required for such an ongoing canonization. The dogmatic function as conventionally conceived is not comprehensive enough to allow the biblical text to speak in all of the ways that the text is able to speak today. The historical approach, while expanding it in certain important directions, limits the potentiality of the text in our day. To emphasize reading and the role of the reader in the process of actualizing the potentiality of the text does not exclude any concern that is conceivable for the reader.

The frame within which the biblical material is placed in a reader centered approach is one that allows it to speak to the reader in a more direct and satisfying way, not simply in an indirect fashion by means of a preliminary reduction to some sort of objective "scientific" data and then an application of that data to human life. The broad role and function of biblical literature, rather than the narrowly conceived original purpose, is the focus. Some original use is not denied, but it is observed that the moment the text was received by the first readers, that limited original use was exhausted. The text then began to be read differently. Readers who were not original recipients made sense in their context with their needs. Our reconceptualizing of biblical texts as literature follows the pattern implicitly followed by readers form the earliest days.

Reader-oriented and Text-oriented

A satisfying role and function of the Bible will emphasize the role of biblical literature in the life of the reader. This does not mean that the text is minimized. On the contrary, the text is taken just as seriously as before. But taking the text seriously in a reader-oriented literary approach does not mean distancing the text so that it becomes and remains ancient and strange. It means situating the text in such a fashion that it is able to speak to the reader in his or her contemporary idiom. At one level, the reader applies a code or group of codes to the text to make sense of the text. In the application of linguistic and literary codes to the text, the reader is assuredly the subject, and the text is the object.

How is it possible for the reader to become the object? Is it possible for the reader to become equal to the text and to "intend" the text for his or her own day? One strategy to effect the move to a reader-oriented approach is to refuse to accept the enabling conditions of biblical texts as the cause and the explanation of those texts. These "causes" may then be seen as past and present devices for reader-meaning rather than as a reduction to historical meaning. There is no need for denial of the fact that certain states of affairs or developments operated in some sense as sources for biblical writings and that biblical writings now reflect those enabling conditions. But attention is to be paid to the realities behind the text (as far as they can be ascertained or imaged) in order to understand the text as a pattern of meaning that continues to have an effect on readers.

Another related strategy is to discern the actual role of the reader in source oriented analysis. Even when the reader appears to be analyzing the text scientifically and discussing the objective structures and causes for such structures, the result of the activity is in part a creative construction of the reader, a construction of cause, which is a result of the effect of the text in the first place. The meanings behind the text and in front of the text coalesce. The various "causes" that criticism has attempted to discern behind the text need not be ignored. They can be reconceptualized in a radical reader-oriented approach as "effects"—the results of the constructive or imaginative work of readers in front of the text, which not only helps them make sense of the text but also coincidentally makes sense of the world and of themselves. "Causes" will not be denied but will be relativized. The historical, sociological, psychological, and other explanations of the text will be seen as legitimate but partial strategies to enable texts to function in helping readers create worlds for themselves intellectually and behaviorally.

The sort of knowledge that is provided by the Bible as literature may be seen as different from the sort of knowledge provided by the Bible as theology or history. This is not simply knowledge of facts that can be determined from the biblical narrative and discourses, detached from the texts, and then reattached to dogmatic and historical systems of the reader's own day. The knowledge gained is the kind that is obtained by viewing biblical texts in the light of their integrity as linguistic and literary creations, by examining the world disclosed in the texts and the world of values and meanings presupposed by the world of the text.

This knowledge may influence the reader more intimately than conventional biblical information. A sensitive reader may, in fact, be "creating" a new world in the process of reading. Readers come to texts and are able to make sense because there is some correlation of textual factors and factors in the reader's world. Characters, events, and situations in the text are not unlike those in the reader's world. But the text often challenges the conceptions and ideologies with which the reader begins, and the reader's world is modified or recreated ideologically. Since world and self do not exist in isolation, however, the reader's self is being redefined in the process. Experience with the text is an experience that alters needs and possibilities. The reader is then creating a world affectively in experience with the text.

The Bible as a Literary Unity

In the process of reading and interpreting a given literary work, it is helpful to place that work in a larger literary context or corpus of works—the works of a particular author, epoch, genre, style, country, and so on. A literary approach to the Bible will benefit from a conceptualization of the literary unity of the Bible. What is the Bible all about as a collection of works of literature? Because of the history of the reception of the Bible, such a conceptualization may be difficult to achieve.

Relativity and Relevance of Earlier Views of the Unity of the Bible

For the ancient and medieval church, the Bible as a whole was the Word of God in terms of a Platonic world view. It could be seen as a result of human linguistic and literary tools, but at a more significant level, the Bible was a sign of God, a communication far above the pitch of human minds. Such a dogmatic view of the unity of the Bible came after the origin and use of biblical writings in the life of Israel and the Christian Church and after the historical process of the Bible's canonization (the Hebrew scriptures in the first century and the Christian scriptures in the fourth century). The biblical writings postulated an "Other" in relation to which the people of God had meaning to be sure. This Other was gracious, and biblical writings were found useful by the community in making known and reenacting his gracious activity. The particular idea of a canon of scripture, defined for the purpose of maintaining integrity in terms of dogma, however, was a result not merely of the genius of the origins and early transmission of the materials but of the world view of the later period, when the canon came to be defined for ecclesiastical purposes.

The development of some concept of the biblical writings as a literary unity could recapitulate the development of the concept of a dogmatic canon. The development of a concept of literary unity could provide a means of reading and appreciating individual writings. Instead of seeing dogmatic relationships, however, literary relationships will be emphasized.

In a new literary conceptualization, some of the literary strategies used to maintain dogmatic presuppositions will be continued—but no longer for the same dogmatic purposes. Medieval exegesis developed strategies that enabled readers to discover different "senses" or layers of meaning in the Bible. Readers acknowledged a literal or historical layer, but they also found an allegorical sense, a tropological sense (referring to the moral meaning), and an analogical sense (the spiritual meaning relating to future and heavenly realities). Typology allowed the early church to maintain the unity of the testaments by understanding earlier events and persons as "types" of later ones. Old Testament events and persons prefigured or foreshadowed their full manifestation in the New Testament. The Exodus could be understood as a type of baptism, and the sacrifice of Isaac could be understood as a type of Christ's sacrifice. Allegory allowed all texts to communicate dogmatic and ethical teachings, even texts that did not obviously or literally have dogmatic or ethical references. Commonplace events and even elements that appear to be morally inferior or even historically questionable could be seen as referring allegorically to God and his will for people.

Specific procedures, found helpful with the dogmatic approach, will be reappropriated in a new literary perspective. The difference will be that the literary strategies will not be at the disposal of a pre-existing dogmatic system but will be employed in the light of literary presuppositions.

With the Enlightenment, the Bible became humanized; the biblical writings were seen as the expression of particular people of particular times and places. History became the key to understanding the unity of the Bible. One external point of reference (dogma) was modified by another. The narrative nature of the Bible made it especially susceptible to accommodation to scientific evolutionary views. This did not rule out dogmatic considerations; it did require dogmatic and historical factors to stand together in a dialectical fashion. In fact, in the nineteenth century, historical study of the Bible was able to assert a religious unity by the idea of "progressive revelation": God revealed his truth as humans were able to understand it. The approach of "biblical theology" in the twentieth century paralleled the earlier approach of "progressive revelation." The Bible was seen as the story of the acts of God in history. With the historical-critical method, then, the Bible assumed a quite different form, in fact, because materials were judged on the basis of their value in the particular historical or historical-religious schema scholars found appropriate. How can the Bible as a whole be viewed today?

Literary Views of Unity: Thematic Unity

The view of the Bible's unity as a dogmatic system was not immediately replaced by the view of the Bible as a historical system. Both systems remained in place. The dogmatic system, however, was no longer validated by a Platonic world view, and interpretation was no longer facilitated by the allegorical approach. The dogmatic view of the Bible was accommodated to a new world view, and methods were validated by that world view. Both of these earlier views of unity constitute the horizon for the construction of a literary view of unity. In fact, one compelling view of the Bible's unity is a translation of the dogmatic/narrative horizon into literary terms.

Northrop Frye says that the form the Bible takes, as he attempts to read it as a totality, is "a gigantic myth, a narrative extending over the whole of time from creation to apocalypse."[10] Hosea 2:18 is the key that allows such unity to be seen in the Bible: "And in that day will I make a covenant for them with the beasts of the field, and with the fowls of heaven, and with the creeping things of the ground: and I will break the bow and the sword and the battle out of the earth, and will make them to lie down safely" (KJV). The Bible is "a vision of upward metamorphosis, of the alienated relation of man to nature transformed into a spontaneous and effortless life—not effortless in the sense of being lazy or passive, but in the sense of being energy without alienation" (*TGC*, p. 76).

> First is the creation, not the natural environment with its alienating chaos but the ordered structure that the mind perceives in it. Next comes the revolutionary vision of human life as a casting off of tyranny and exploitation. Next is the ceremonial, moral, judicial code that keeps a society together. Next is the wisdom or sense of integrated continuous life which grows out of this, and next the prophecy or imaginative vision of man as somewhere between his original and his ultimate identity. Gospel and apocalypse speak of a present that no longer finds its meaning in the future, as in the New Testament's view of the Old Testament, but is a present moment around which past and future resolve. (*TGC*, pp. 224-25)

From one perspective, the mythic unity of the Bible results from the narrative nature of the Bible and an evolutionary ideology. Even though the seven phases (creation, revolution or exodus, law, wisdom, prophecy, gospel, and apocalypse) are not to be seen simply in an evolutionary way so that each phase is an improvement on its predecessor, there is development in that each phase is a wider perspective on its predecessor. Each phase is "a type of the one following it and an antitype of the one preceding it" (*TGC*, p. 106).

From another perspective, the conception of "upward metamorphosis" as the basis of biblical unity is a literary explanation of the historical fact of a continuous reinterpretation and rewriting of biblical materials within the Bible itself. The sequence of the Bible is thereby related to its capacity for self-recreation. The formation of the Pentateuch reveals "a highly self-conscious retrospective view of the early history of Israelite culture." The chronicler's recreation of Samuel and Kings, the psalmist's recreation of the Exodus experience in such psalms as 78 and 106, the assimilation of later periods of bondage in exile to earlier ones, and (for the reader of the Christian Bible) the complete reconstruction of the Old Testament in the New are examples of the Bible's capacity for self-recreation.

> The dialectical expansion from one "level" of understanding to another seems to be built into the Bible's own structure, which creates an awareness of itself by the reader, growing in time as he reads, to an extent to which I can think of no parallel elsewhere. Nor can we trace the Bible back to a time when it was not doing this. (*TGC*, p. 225)

The myth of upward metamorphosis as the basis for unification is accompanied by a view of "the body of the Messiah" as the point of unification. The recurring imagery of the Bible " 'freezes' into a single metaphor cluster, the metaphors all being identified with the body of the Messiah, the man who is all men, the totality of *logoi* who is one Logos, the grain of sand that is the world" (*TGC*, p. 224). In the New Testament, this "speaking presence in history" is identified as the "Christ." When the Bible and the person of Christ are identified metaphorically, the phrase "Word (Logos) of God" may be used of the Bible. But this is legitimate only as the referential or centrifugal meaning of the Bible is subordinated to a primary centripetal meaning.[11]

The unity of the Bible envisioned by Frye is in part a result of Frye's own literary world view, one driven toward unity and unification. It is consciously influenced by the fact that the Bible that is important for Frye (and "for English literature of the Western cultural tradition generally") is the Christian Bible "with its polemically named 'Old' and 'New' Testaments" (*TGC*, p. xiii). Some contemporary approaches do not presuppose and seek such unity, and some biblical scholars could see Frye's evolutionary framework to be the remnants of a Christian triumphalism. Is it possible to reconceptualize the rich biblical data so as to maintain a unity while not allowing the narrative nature of the text and an evolutionary ideology to lead to a view of progression from inferior to superior? It is possible to view what Frye sees as a sequence and procession of recreations more as a group of exclusive systems standing in opposition to one another. If so, how can unity be imposed on such exclusive systems?

Michael Fishbane sees the same constructions that Frye sees in the Hebrew scriptures not simply as a sequence but as competing views and "multiple structures of reality" that are mutually exclusive. His view of the unity of the Hebrew scriptures may be useful also in a reconceptualization of the Christian scriptures (the New Testament in relation to the Hebrew scriptures). According to Fishbane, not only has the true fulfillment of the Hebrew Bible been seen alternatively in *Nomos*, prophecy, *Ethos*, and *Mythos*, but the contest between these opposing truths has been one conducted "in deathly earnest." Proclamation of one truth has been seen as excluding others. "The outsider was peremptorily hounded, excluded and ejected." The Bible itself, then, sponsors constructions of the sacred that are mutually exclusive.[12]

The unity that is to be seen from such a perspective is different from Frye's; it is a "concordant discord." The discord, of course, results from the exclusive views of sacrality; the concord results from the fact that these exclusive views are all included in the same Bible. The Bible may be seen as a "conveyor of sacrality" in and through the very contestations the Bible records. The Bible, therefore, is not only a maker of exclusive views, but it is also a breaker of such exclusive views in its containment of those views. The biblical text in its entirety is a "prophetic eruption" in its own right. The Bible as a whole neutralizes "the competing claims of contrasting interbiblical and postbiblical ideologies."[13]

The sacredness sponsored by the Bible, then, comes to be the result of a vision that provides an opening to transcendence by seeing in the Bible a model for a plurality of visions of multiform humanity. "The sacrality released hereby would not be the competitive sacrality of segregated symbols. Rather, this new Bible-sponsored sacrality would allow the awesome transcendence of the divine reality to chasten our constructions of order and sacrality."[14] Fishbane proposes that the biblical anthology of differences sponsors the "eruption of a prophetic voice critical of the potential dangers of human symbolic systems." The Bible, then, would relativize the idols of the human *textus*, but this relativizing is "for the sake of the transcendent divine *textus*."[15]

The views of the Bible as a series evolving from creation to apocalypse or as a series of competing truths are influenced by a diachronic perspective and the historically constrained form of the dogmatic content of the Bible. These views must be challenged or at least relativized by criticism of evolutionary views going back to discussion of "progressive revelation." In the 1960s Alan Richardson suggested:

> Recent biblical research would lead us to hesitate before we speak of the insights even of the great prophets as being 'higher' than those of the J writer (or 'tradition') in Genesis; did not J present in his own 'primitive' way an insight as profound, as ultimate, as anything which we find in the Deutero-Isaiah, even though he clothed it in childlike, pictorial language? The truth would seem to be rather that insights into God's character and into man's relationship with God are independent of relative priority or lateness in an evolutionary series. . . . There is a sense in which, though there is progress in scientific knowledge, there is not necessarily an equivalent progress in men's existential awareness of their personal being as standing over against, yet in the presence of, their creator, who commands their obedience.[16]

A structuralist perspective, which gives attention to "deep" as well as to "superficial" levels, could emphasize the continuity existing at a profound level throughout the series of competing systems. This profound continuity may be appreciated by examining the unity of the Bible not in terms of dogmatic content but in terms of literary structure.

The relativizing emphasized by Fishbane, then, would be accompanied by a relativizing of dogmatic content of each of the series in the light of the poetic content and meaning of the Bible as a whole.

Literary Views of Unity: Unity of Style

The Bible can be read and interpreted in a literary context instead of explicit dogmatic and/or historical contexts because the Bible shares characteristics of all of literature. The normal practice of maintaining the poetic aspect of the Bible separate from literature in general (a practice followed by Samuel Johnson in his canons of criticism) is not legitimate. It unnecessarily limits the potentiality of biblical literature. Once the point is made that the Bible is literature, however, it is possible to see that the biblical writings share a common literary shape.

The biblical writings share a common narrative plot at the most profound level. This common plot may be perceived by utilizing the fourfold organization of basic motifs, or "pre-generic elements of literature," at work prior to the development of ordinary literary genres. (The four seasons of the year have been used in explicating the motifs.) These elements are comedy (the Mythos of Spring), romance (the Mythos of Summer), tragedy (the Mythos of Autumn), and irony and satire (the Mythos of Winter).[17] The Bible contains stories that reflect all of these plots and their modifications and combination. Romance is the successful quest, and the complete form of the romance has a preliminary stage of a perilous journey with its minor adventures, a crucial struggle in which either the hero or his foe or both must die, and the exaltation of the hero, who has proved himself to be a hero even if he does not survive the conflict. Abraham's quest for a son and Ruth's quest for a home represent romance. The books of Esther and Jonah and the materials in Daniel 1–6 share characteristics of romance.

Tragedy is an account of the events in the life of a person of significance that culminate in an unhappy catastrophe. Tragedy is the mimesis of sacrifice in the sense that it is "a paradoxical combination of a fearsome sense of rightness (the hero must fall) and a pitying sense of wrongness (it is too bad that he falls)" (*AC*, p. 214). The incongruous and the inevitable are combined in tragedy. In his *Anatomy of Criticism,* Frye indicates that the archetype of the inevitably ironic in terms of tragedy is Adam, "human nature under sentence of death." On the other hand, the archetype of the incongruously ironic is Christ, "the perfectly innocent victim excluded from human society" (*AC*, p. 42). Halfway between these two is "the central figure of tragedy, who is human and yet of a heroic size which often has in it the suggestion of divinity." Prometheus is the archetype of this central figure of tragedy, "the immortal titan rejected by the gods for befriending men." Although he tries to make himself into a tragic Promethean figure by justifying himself as a victim of God, Job does not succeed. The book of Job, then, "is not a tragedy of the Promethian type, but a tragic irony in which the dialectic of the divine and the human nature works itself out" (*AC*, p. 42). Irony and satire are based on the sense that heroism and effective action are absent, disorganized, or doomed to defeat; reigning over the world are confusion and anarchy. The standard shape of comedy is a U-shaped pattern in which the action is first of all brought to a low point by a series of misfortunes and then sent to a happy conclusion by some fortunate twist in the plot. The normal pattern of action for comedy is the desire of a young man for a young woman, resistance of this desire by some opposition, and a twist near the end of the plot, which enables the hero to have his will. (See *AC*, p. 163; *TGC*, p. 169.)

Although the Bible contains examples of the different plots, the thrust of the Bible is in the direction of the comic. This does not mean that romance, irony, and especially tragedy are not involved, but they are not central. Tragedy is seen in Christianity, for example, as an essential episode in the larger scheme of the divine comedy, which involves redemption and resurrection. "The sense of tragedy as a prelude to comedy seems almost inseparable from anything explicitly Christian" (*AC*, p. 215). Illustrations from music help make the point.

> The serenity of the final double chorus in the St. Matthew Passion would hardly be attainable if composer and audience did not know that there was more to the story. Nor would the death of Samson lead to "calm of mind, all passion spent," if Samson were not a prototype of the rising Christ, associated at the appropriate moment with the phoenix. (*AC*, p. 215)

Readers of the Bible must also make sense of tragic moments in the light of the essentially comic direction of the Bible as a whole—the Hebrew and Christian scriptures.

The comic pattern is obvious in the stories of the failure, captivity, and redemption of the People of God. But an essentially comic perspective is also evident in the non-narrative material of the Bible. The book of Isaiah is seen by historical critics as separate oracles, representing different historical moments in Israel's life. From the perspective of the comic plot, however, Isaiah may be seen as a unity. This unity is "not of authorship but of theme, and that theme in epitome the theme of the Bible as a whole, as the parable of Israel lost, captive, and redeemed" (*AC*, p. 56).

The poetics of the Bible, with its comic plot, is related to its particular world picture.

> Given God's relation to man, [the Bible] must propel the characters toward enlightenment: to spread knowledge, influence choice, validate the election of learners, justify the fate of backsliders, as well as to guarantee the foolproof composition whereby not even the slowest in the uptake among the audience will be left unenlightened at the end. And in the interests of rhetorical effect, it must preserve the greatest freedom in manipulating the reader's journey and the least freedom in establishing his terminus, which in principle coincides with that of the better sort of characters. . . . Within these limits . . . enough can be achieved by way of complication, ambiguity, play if you will, to satisfy the most fastidious. But the limits themselves, whether viewed as ideological or rhetorical premises, are sacrosanct. For to violate them would be to undermine the very idea of divine order: that the world is intelligible, because providentially con-

trolled, however mysterious if not offensive its workings may appear to dim eyes. (*PBN*, p. 179)[18]

The Bible not only has a unity in terms of an essential plot related to ideology, but it also has a common shape in terms of concrete images. Positive images that appear and reappear include the bride, the shepherd, the wedding, the feast, bread, wine, sheep, garden, mountain, vineyard, river, and wind. Negative images include the drunkard, slavery, sackcloth, disease, hunger, the cave, weeds, desert, the sea, the storm, and weeping and wailing.[19] It is possible to arrange the concrete images in terms of the comic view, with the negative elements dominating when misfortunes bring the action to a low point and the positive elements dominating when a fortunate twist in the plot brings about a happy ending. To an extent, major positive images (characters such as Abraham, Moses, Joshua, Ruth, the Judges, David, Ezra and Nehemiah, John the Baptist, Jesus, Peter; localities such as Eden, the promised land, Jerusalem, the temple, and so on) are related metaphorically to one another, as are the major negative images (the Pharaoh of the Exodus, Nebuchadnezzar, and Antiochus Epiphanes; Egypt, Babylon, and Rome; see *TGC*, p. 171.)

Recurring type-scenes create a unity in the Bible. These exist as microstructures and macrostructures. Biblical scholars are familiar with the microstructures, or "forms," that have been emphasized by form critics—such type-scenes as healing stories and pronouncement stories. These type-scenes consist of conventional elements, often in a set order. The same phenomenon exists on a broader level, and these macroscopic type-scenes may be just as helpful as the smaller forms in creating a literary unity of the Bible. Robert Alter identifies the following as biblical type-scenes: "the annunciation . . . of the birth of the hero to his barren mother; the encounter with the future betrothed at a well; the epiphany in the field; the initiatory trial; danger in the desert and the discovery of a well or other source of sustenance; the testament of the dying hero."[20] Once we become sensitive to such typical scenes or series of actions, we may see more and more such phenomena. The well-known cycle in the book of Judges may be seen as growing out of a type-scene governed by a particular ideology of the relationship between sin and suffering. National apostasy results in enslavement, but repentance results in deliverance. Deliverance, however, is followed by national apostasy, and so on. It is possible to view the book of the Acts of the Apostles in similar terms: God raises up leaders who preach the gospel and perform mighty works; crowds are drawn, and people are converted; the leaders face opposition and persecution; God intervenes to rescue; and so on.[21]

Attention to the use of the same literary form and imagery in different literary writings enables readers to move beyond the practice of perceiving each writing as a separate center of scholarship (see *AC*, p. 342). This is valid for biblical literature. Reading individual biblical writings in the light of a biblical "language" leads to greater appreciation of those particular writings as literature, but concern with the biblical "language" itself may lead to a discovery of a general literary "message."

Mathematics has been used as an analogy to assist conceptualization and appreciation of literature as a language. Mathematics normally appears as a numerical commentary on the outside world in its function in the counting and measuring of objects. But in a certain sense, mathematics is an autonomous language that may become independent of the objective world. "Many of its terms, such as irrational numbers, have no direct connection with the common field of experience, but depend for their meaning solely on the interrelations of the subject itself." Literature parallels mathematics in that even though it is first thought of as a commentary on the external world, it can move from reflection of life to become an autonomous language (*AC*, pp. 350-51). The autonomous language of literature may be thought of as itself representing a truth.

> Poets and critics alike have always believed in some kind of imaginative truth, and perhaps the justification for the belief is in the containment by the language of what it can express. The mathematical and the verbal universes are doubtless different ways of conceiving the same universe. The objective world affords a provisional means of unifying experience, and it is natural to infer a higher unity, a sort of beatification of common sense. But it is not easy to find any language capable of expressing the unity of this higher intellectual universe. . . . Whenever we construct a system of thought to unite earth with heaven, the story of the Tower of Babel recurs; we discover that after all we can't quite make it, and that what we have in the meantime is a plurality of languages. (*AC*, p. 354)

The vision of a unified intellectual universe is found compelling by Frye. He postulates that this unity is a literary creation itself, requiring an actualization by the critic or the "ideal reader." The last chapter of *Finnegans Wake* is used to explicate the task of the reforging of "the broken links between creation and knowledge, art and science, myth and concept." The dreamer in that last chapter spends the night in communion with a vast body of metaphorical identifications. When he wakens, however, he goes about his business forgetting his dream, like Nebuchadnezzar, "failing to use, or even to realize that he can use, the 'keys to dreamland.' " What the dreamer fails to do is left for the reader to do. "The 'ideal reader suffering from an ideal insomnia,' as Joyce calls him, in other words the critic" (*AC*, p. 354).

When the biblical text is seen as playing its part in the creation of the world of the reader, the view of the Bible as a special sort of language may become relevant. The particular texts and their concrete actions, characters, and situations are important not only as individual writings but also as the vehicle for a comprehensive "language" in which all the other particular texts with their concrete phenomena play a part.

How does the Bible as language relate to the language of literature in general? The Bible may be seen as representing one of the two major aspects of a "mythological universe." One aspect of the total mythological universe is our own creation, "man's vision of his own life as a quest." Secular stories form this single integrated vision of the world, and romance is the structural core of the fiction that forms the "epic of the creature." But another aspect of this mythological universe is what is considered traditionally as "a revelation given to man by God or other powers beyond himself." This is "the epic of the creator, with God as its hero."[22] Both aspects are vital for our activities as men and women:

> It is quite true that if there is no sense that the mythological universe is a human creation, man can never get free of servile anxieties and superstitions, never surpass himself, in Nietzsche's phrase. But if there is no sense that it is also something uncreated, something coming from elsewhere, man remains a Narcissus staring at his own reflection, equally unable to surpass himself. Somehow or other, the created scripture and the revealed scripture, or whatever we call the latter, have to keep fighting each other like Jacob and the angel, and it is through the maintaining of this struggle, the suspension of belief between the spiritually real and the humanly imaginative, that our own mental evolution grows.[23]

When the Bible is seen as "the epic of the creator," the reader's interaction with biblical texts may result in a special kind of knowledge. It is a knowledge of what it means to be human, but this knowledge is different from that obtained from reading of secular romance. The knowledge a reader attains at the end of his or her sustained effort is "the knowledge of our limitations." This is "the only knowledge perfectly acquired." But the attainment of this is the attainment of "something of the vision that God has possessed all along." It is because of this that "to make sense of the discourse is to gain a sense of being human" (*PBN*, p. 47).[24]

The chastening of human constructions of order

and sacrality, which Michael Fishbane sees as the role of the Bible in our day, is positive in that movement is made beyond any one of the "opposing truths" of the Bible to a sacrality that affects the creation of our world as individuals and as a people. The emphasis on the poetic structures and content and their relativizing of superficial dogmatic content arrives at the same conclusion as to the function of the Bible in our lives as individuals and as a society.

A role for biblical literature that grows out of this vision is a reader-oriented role. In terms of the private realm, "the Bible may become sacred to us as fragments of its images and language shape our discourse; provide dialectical antithesis for our moral and spiritual growth; and simply bind us to past generations which also took this multiform document seriously." The Bible, together with other texts, "helps establish our personhood and outline our possibilities . . . it may help us to transcend older visions and propose newer ones; and . . . the Bible may provide the words and values through which we may cross-over from the private to the interhuman realm."[25]

When individuals share this vision and "speak out of their private worlds of antithetical fragments and hesitant images," a public function is carried out: "a realization of the partiality and limitations of every attempt to decode the divine reality." The common sharing of verbalizations of reality lead to a realization of transcendence, a reality that may be alluded to by human language but "forever eludes these imaginable constructions." Fishbane suggests that "the ultimate sacral possibility of the Bible may . . . lie in providing a dim realization of the radical Otherness of divine transcendence to all linguistic pretensions to meaning." In this process, "the Bible itself, with its own pretension to present a humanly conditioned divine voice, would also be radically transcended."[26]

Imaging the Divine

In approaching the Bible as literature, readers have not dispensed with powers beyond themselves, with the uncreated, with the sacred. A literary approach means that the sacred is approached not in dogmatic terms (in terms of particular dogmatic and ecclesiastical systems) but in terms of language and literary creation. A literary approach may allow a vision of Otherness or Transcendence that does not necessitate accepting the embarrassing theological baggage of the past. A contemporary imaging of the sacred, however, will also take a skeptical attitude toward models of language and knowledge that methodologically exclude divinity.

The Divine and Developments in Language

Rudolf Bultmann declared that as a result of science and technology, we have lost the capacity to conceive of the divine. Bultmann took it as an uncontested rule that the knowledge proved by modern science and the *faith* engendered by that science had brought religious faith into discord with itself insofar as God is concerned. The expression "death of God" is used to describe this experience of the loss of biblical transcendence.[27]

From a contemporary postcritical perspective, the problem of conceiving of the divine may be seen as the result of developments in language, whereby the prevailing model of language (and its presuppositions) is at odds with biblical models of language and those presuppositions. God may not so much be dead as "entombed in a dead language" (*TGC*, p. 18). God's linguistic entombment, then, would be a result of the rise to domination of the descriptive phase of language, in which the ideal to be achieved by words is framed on the model of truth by correspondence. Truth is related to an external source, which is used as a criterion for judgment. In such a model of language, no validation is provided for God because of the absence of an external source. God cannot be conceived of in such a model. Even though this is a result of the model and its presuppositions, for those whose world is defined by the model, there is no room for God.

The Divine in Earlier Phases of Language. The descriptive phase of language is only one phase. In two earlier phases of language, the divine was not only conceivable but also was essential. In the poetic, or metaphoric, phase, there is a sense of identity between humankind and nature in terms of life or power or energy. Subject and object are not essentially separate but are linked by this common power. The identity of personality and nature is embodied in the divine. A "verbal magic" arises from the sense of an energy that is common to words and things. This energy is embodied and controlled in words.

When a sacrosanct myth is read at a religion festival, as, say the Babylonian creation myth *Enuma elish* was read at the New Year, some kind of magical energy is clearly being released. It would perhaps be overconceptualizing to say that it was thought to encourage the natural cycle to keep turning for another year; but where the subject and the object are not clearly separated, and there are forms of energy common to both, a controlled and articulated expression of words may have repercussions in the natural order. (*TGC,* pp. 7-8)

The second phase of language is one in which words are conceived of as the outward expression of inner thoughts or ideas. There is a consistent separation of subject and object. The sense of *identity* of life between humankind and nature characteristic of the poetic phase ("this is that"), is exchanged for a sense of metonymic *relationship* ("this is put for that").

Specifically, words are "put for" thoughts, and are the outward expressions of an inner reality. But this reality is not merely "inside." Thoughts indicate the existence of a transcendent order "above," with which only thinking can communicate and which only words can express. Thus, metonymic language is, or tends to become, analogical language, a verbal imitation of a reality beyond itself that can be conveyed most directly by words. (*TGC,* p. 6)

In the second phase, the unifying conception becomes a transcendent reality or a perfect being. All verbal analogy points to this monotheistic God. Medieval fascination with the syllogism and the dream of the deduction of all knowledge from the premise of revelation grow out of this phase of language.

Analogical language thus came to be thought of as sacramental language, a verbal response to God's own verbal revelation. Some form of analogy was essential, otherwise there would be no reality that human language is "put for," and no one would maintain that human language was fully adequate to conveying such a reality. (*TGC*, pp. 11-12)[28]

Biblical Language and Earlier Phases of Language. The view of language represented in the Bible cannot really be equated with the various phases of language discussed here. It certainly cannot be equated with the descriptive phase, but the Platonic and Neoplatonic view of the second phase is also inappropriate, for the biblical God is not divorced from the world to be discerned only in a reflective process.[29] The poetic phase of language as such is inappropriate for appreciating the Bible, since, for the Bible, God is not simply to be *identified* with the world. It was through his Word that God created the world. Shemaryahu Talmon has argued that the form of biblical narrative is a deliberate avoidance of the epic of paganism for ideological reasons.

The ancient Hebrew writers purposefully nurtured and developed prose narration to take the place of the epic genre which by its content was intimately bound up with the world of paganism, and appears to have had a special standing in the polytheistic cults. The recitation of the epics was tantamount to an enactment of cosmic events in the manner of sympathetic magic. In the process of total rejection of the polytheistic religions and their ritual expressions in the cult, epic songs and also the epic genre were purged from the repertoire of the Hebrew authors.[30]

Biblical texts may not be seen simply in the light of the first phase of language, in which a quasi-physical power is released by speech, causing repercussions in the natural order. Yet, there is a parallel between the poetic phase and biblical language. In biblical language, there is a power in the words. It is not addressed to the natural world. It is directed to the hearers/readers and is designed to have a repercussion in their lives. Narrative addressed to the people of God does not merely recount what happened in the lives of their ancestors. There is not simply a historical and an exegetical "telling" on the part of the narrator; there is also a dramatic "showing." The narrator unfolds a history "grounded in God's control and providence, enjoining a remembrance of his wonders from Creation onward, with the Exodus as a focal point, and therefore inextricably bound to a sense of the past" (*PBN,* p. 45).

The direct citation of God's performance is in effect a dramatic "showing" in which the "seeing" on the part of the descendants of the audience in the original drama effects a reenactment of the acts being shown. "Indeed, considering the role played by 'seeing' in that process of transmission, dramatic 'showing' gains priority as the technique that comes closest to reenacting for the sons the marvelous acts originally eyewitnessed by the fathers" (*PBN,* p. 122).

Beyond the Descriptive Phase of Language. The third phase of language arose roughly in the sixteenth century because of the perception that syllogistic reasoning and analogical language did not deal with realities. Syllogistic reasoning could lead to nothing really new because its conclusions were contained in its premises. The march of syllogistic reasoning across reality, then, was merely a verbal illusion. The analogical approach to language, on the other hand, lacked criteria for distinguishing what genuinely exists from what does not exist in reality.

> Grammatically, logically, and syntactically, there is no difference between a lion and a unicorn: the question of actual existence does not enter the ordering of words as such. And if it does not, there can be no real difference between reasoning and rationalizing, as both procedures order words in the same way. The difference can be established only by criteria external to words, and the first of these criteria has to be that of "things" or objects in nature. (*TGC*, pp. 12-13)

In the third phase, therefore, the criterion of reality is the order of nature as the source of sense experience. This criterion means that "'God' is not to be found and . . . 'gods' are no longer believed in. Hence for the third phase of language the word 'God' becomes linguistically unfunctional, except when confined to special areas outside its jurisdiction" (*TGC*, p. 15).

The fact that we are able to see "the death of God" as the entombment of God in a dead language, which does not necessarily reflect "reality," may be evidence that language has moved beyond the third phase. Contemporary criticism, indeed, is seen in this volume as in part a conflict between modern and postmodern philosophies and strategies, with "modern" referring to ideas related to the third phase of language described above, and "postmodern" emphasizing the limitation of that sort of human rationality. The assumptions of the third phase of language concerning the human being (the subject), the world (object), the rational process and truth are questioned.[31]

The loss of stability thought to exist in the foundationalist Western philosophical system need not lead to despair and nihilism. The deconstructive move reveals that we are in a new stage—but one which is developing against the horizon of the descriptive phase which remains in place. Any new phase will be one which acknowledges the limitations of the subject-object dicotomy and the philosophical and theological presuppositions and conclusions related to the division.

Contemporary developments in language may be viewed positively. Einstein may be seen as the forerunner of a new view.[32] With Einstein, the sense of the clear scientific separation of subject and object began to come to an end. No longer was it possible to separate the observer from the observed; the observer is also the observed.

> The thought suggests itself that we may have completed a gigantic cycle of language from Homer's time, where the word evokes the thing, to our own day, where the thing evokes the word, and are now about to go around the cycle again, as we seem now to be confronted once again with an energy common to subject and object which can be expressed verbally only through some form of metaphor. It is true that many metaphorical elements are reappearing in our language, but it is rather the positive aspect of the same process—that we may be entering a new phase altogether in our understanding of language—that has to be kept in mind. (*TGC*, p. 15)

Is it possible that in the new phase of language, God may be conceptualized once again? In the second phase of language, the use of the word *God* as a noun, which fits into the category of things and objects, presented no logical problem. God represented an immutable being, set in opposition to human experience of "the dissolving flow of the world of becoming." The appropriate grammatical device for conveying this immutability was the abstract noun. The view of God as a noun (a being, even though an immutable being) in the second phase of language made the elimination of God in the third phase inevitable. This is because the noun *God* has no reference in the natural world, and the natural world had become the criterion for reality and the basis for language in the descriptive phase. There is no particular being to which the word refers. Reconceptualizing God in verbal, rather than substantive, terms may be more consistent with the Bible.

> This would involve trying to think our way back to a conception of language in which words were words of power, conveying primarily the sense of forces and energies rather than analogues of physical bodies. To some extent this would be a reversion to the metaphorical language of primitive communities. . . . But it would also be oddly contemporary with post-Einsteinian physics, where atoms and electrons are no longer thought of as things but rather as traces of processes. God may have lost his function as the subject or object of a predicate, but may not be so much dead as entombed in a dead language. (*TGC,* pp. 17-18)

The Divine and the Language of Existence

The conceiving of the divine in a postmodern phase of language may be advanced by the work of

John Macquarrie, whose theology is based on antifoundationalist philosophical thought. Macquarrie is not interested in giving philosophical and theological support to the idea of the God of classical theism. He feels that we have moved beyond the idea of God as the *being* who created the world, who exercises governance over the world, and who intervenes in his creation on occasions. Nevertheless Macquarrie believes that human experience is fulfilled in communion with a reality that transcends human existence. Moreover, Macquarrie desires to provide a satisfactory account of that reality in terms that are faithful to the Bible and to contemporary conceptual thought and language. For Macquarrie, that language is the language of existence and being. He recognizes that theological discourse arises from a religious discourse whose roots are in a pre-theological language, the language of mythology. Mythical language has its own vivid power of communication, which is "still exploited by novelists and dramatists in a post-mythical age." Instead of investigating the possibility of moving beyond the limitations of the third phase of language, Macquarrie opts for translating and interpreting the meanings and significances expressed in the earlier pre-theological language into the language of the third, or descriptive, phase. The influence of Bultmann's view of myth and modern humanity on Macquarrie helps us understand this aim.

We ourselves live in a post-mythical age. . . . With the rise of science, the background of presuppositions on which mythical discourse proceeded has been gradually destroyed. Thus modern man finds that myth does not communicate to him, for the condition that language may communicate is precisely that one shares a frame of reference with the person who uses the language.

Macquarrie indicates that "perhaps the modern man can still catch something of the evocative and allusive character of the myth, and suspect that in spite of its apparent absurdities, it may contain insights that remain valid and are not to be dismissed as just primitive superstition." Nevertheless a new act of interpretation is necessary for eliciting these insights. The new act of interpretation will allow the insights of the myth to be expressed in a language that can communicate in a post-mythical world. "It may be that in the end, after such an interpretation has been offered, one can go back to the myth with a new appreciation," but the fact that the myth is now recognized as myth makes the present attitude different from the "archaic mentality that lived in the as yet undifferentiated myth." Nevertheless "if an interpretive key has been found, the dramatic form of the myth may be found to communicate its insight with a forcefulness that would not belong to an abstract language."[33]

The assumption of this volume is that the hope hinted at by Macquarrie is becoming a reality, that a contemporary approach to biblical texts will open up those texts to direct appreciation without a detour through any philosophical system. Nevertheless some readers may wish to express this literary experience of transcendence in terms more clearly suited to a critical language, and Macquarrie's critical language may meet this desire and thereby assist their literary imaging of the divine.

Macquarrie acknowledges that the language of the Bible and of religion in general expresses religious faith and that neither the language of the Bible nor the faith expressed by that language is reducible to propositions. Nevertheless faith is not unrelated to the cognitive dimensions of human life. Although religious language expresses subjective emotion, it goes beyond mere feeling in that "these affective elements are inseparable from what are believed to be insights into the way things are." Macquarrie uses Ian Ramsey's idea that religious language involves not only "commitment" but also "discernment." Were no discernment expressed in the religious language, the commitment would constitute bigotry or fanaticism. Religious language, then, is "the vehicle for understanding and insight, so that it tells us something." But what does it tell us? What does religious language light up for us?[34] To answer the question of the reference of religious language (beyond feeling and valuation), Macquarrie uses Martin Heidegger's concept of being as "the *transcendens* pure and simple." Being is the condition for beings. As such, it is not an entity; it is the act by which things are. Macquarrie suggests that Exodus 3:14 might be translated as: "I let be what I let be." God *is* in a dynamic and creative sense. Rather than describe God as "he who is," we might better describe God as "he who lets be."

Being is . . . a *transcendens* which, as above all categories, must remain mysterious, and yet is not just a blank incomprehensible. The very fact that it is the condition that there may be any beings or properties of beings is an indication that although we cannot say of being that it "is," and might even say it is "nothing that is," being "is" nevertheless more beingful than anything that is, for it is the prior condition that anything may be."[35]

The language of faith refers to being not as an object, but "being as known in the revelatory experience."[36] The religious person claims that faith is made possible "by the initiative of that toward which" faith is directed. The religious individual's "*quest* for the sense of existence is met by the *gift* of the sense for existence."

He experiences this initiative from beyond himself in various ways. In so far as it supports and strengthens his existence and helps to overcome its fragmentariness and impotence, he calls the gift that comes to him "grace." In so far as it lays claim on him and exposes the distortions of his existence, it may be called "judgment." In so far as it brings him a new understanding both of himself and of the wider being within which he has his being (for the understanding of these is correlative), then it may be called "revelation." The word "revelation" points therefore especially to the cognitive element in the experience.[37]

Although faith is not just an arbitrary decision, "one cannot get behind the experience of the grace of being to know whether this is a valid experience or an illusory one. All that can be done is to offer a description of the experience, indeed, to trace it all the way from its sources in the way our human existence is constituted." This limitation, this inability to replace faith by certitude, is tied up with our destiny as finite beings, our need "to commit ourselves in one way or another without conclusive proof."[38]

The language of faith, then, refers simultaneously to an insight into the way things are, to being, which is understood both as gracious and as the source of meaning within existence, and to a commitment to this being, understood as gracious. Since being is not an object and cannot be referred to in direct and straightforward ways, language must be stretched beyond its normal usage. (Macquarrie here is thinking of language in the third phase.) When the language of religion is taken in a literal sense, it is utterly misunderstood. The language points perhaps ostensibly to some particular being; yet, the language is opening a way into an understanding of being. The necessity for this stretching of language beyond its normal usages is plain: "Being is not a being, but since our language is adapted to talking about beings, then we must talk of Being in the language appropriate to beings." Macquarrie justifies this use of language in the idea that Being is present and manifest in beings and that "it is only in and through beings (including our own being) that we can have any understanding of Being. The presence and manifestation of Being in beings, or, alternatively expressed, the participation of beings in Being, justifies the logic of a language of beings that has been stretched to serve as a language of Being."[39]

Is it possible that the movement to a concept of language unconstrained by the presuppositions of the third stage of language will enable contemporary readers to appreciate biblical texts in a way comparable to the experience of the earliest readers?

In Frye's concept of a new stage of language, no complete return is made to the first stage of language and to pantheism. But what would be the relationship between deity and the world? Macquarrie's work may help us envision this relationship in a new stage of language and thought. Macquarrie distinguishes his view from pantheism because he does not feel that God is exhausted by the universe. Traditional ideas of God's transcendence and priority, however, are qualified by a view of God's relation to the world. God and world are distinguishable but not separable. The interdependence of God and world means that God is not to be conceived of apart from creation: God affects creation but is also in some sense affected by creation. Eugene Thomas Long indicates that it is this idea that distinguishes Macquarrie's idea of God from the concept of God in classical theism.

> What Macquarrie proposes is a theory of God that stresses the infinite temporality of God and the intimate relation between God and world without foregoing the emphasis on God's transcendence. God is understood by Macquarrie as Being, the *transcendens,* who is nevertheless in the world in relation to persons and things. God is understood as the Being of beings, or the form of the world, who in his structure is related to his creation. As my being in the world in relation to persons and things is not accidental to my being, so God's being in the world in relation to persons and things is not accidental to God. The relation of God to his creation is part of the essential structure of God.[40]

The language of analogy in religion is related to Macquarrie's view of pantheism because such language refers to a situation in which God discloses himself as in the world and as transcending the world. We are not directed, therefore, merely to the words spoken but to the situation to which the words are spoken. The "Word of God," therefore, expresses God as he is disclosed to the one who hears his Word and not God as he is in himself. As Long says, "The words and actions which mediate our relation to God, which give insight into the nature of God as he is for us, are related to God in the way that the words and actions of a person are related to him when he reveals himself to us. Analogues express or give insight into the nature of God, but God is not identical with these expressions."[41]

Notes

1. Jurij Lotman, *The Structure of the Artistic Text*, Michigan Slavic Contributions 7, trans. Gail Lenhoff and Ronald Vroon (Ann Arbor: University of Michigan Press, 1977), pp. 23-24.

2. T. S. Eliot, *The Use of Poetry and the Use of Criticism* (Cambridge, Mass: Harvard University Press, 1933), p. 153. Cited in Meir Sternberg, *The Poetics of Biblical Narrative*, p. 50.

3. Historiography mediates between ideology and aesthetics because of the twofold bearing of biblical history. "On the one hand, this history unfolds a theology in action—one distinctly grounded in God's control and providence. . . . On the other hand, this history makes a story and therefore not only accommodates but also co-determines the rules of narrative" (*PBN*, pp. 44-45).

4. Meir Sternberg's emphasis on the Bible as history rather than literature seems at first glance to challenge a literary approach; in fact, however, his position confirms a reader-oriented literary approach. Sternberg is so determined that the historiographic principle regulating biblical narrative not be

lost that he is cautious in using the term *literary* of biblical narrative without careful qualification, and he roundly condemns Robert Alter's description of biblical narrative as "prose fiction." For Sternberg, biblical narrative is history, not fiction! History and fiction are to be distinguished not on the basis of the relationship of the text to what "really happened," but on the basis of purpose, claim, or commitment. History writing, therefore, is not necessarily a record of fact; it is "a discourse that claims to be a record of fact." Fiction writing, on the other hand, is not necessarily an inventive text; it is "a discourse that claims freedom of invention" (*PBN*, p. 25).

5. Stephen A. Geller, "Were the Prophets Poets?" *Prooftexts: A Journal of Jewish Literary History* 3 (1983):219-20.

6. James L. Kugel, "On the Bible and Literary Criticism," *Prooftexts: A Journal of Jewish Literary History* 1 (1981):219. All excerpts from this work copyright © 1981. Used by permission of Johns Hopkins University Press.

7. Ibid., p. 233.

8. Kugel compares contemporary literary criticism of the Bible with the rabbinic approach to scripture known as *midrash*. The midrashic approach to scripture assumed its omnisignificance—that is, it assumed "that every particularity of the Bible's manner of expression is there to tell us something, and that there is no such thing as mere repetition, restatement, or emphasis, no contradiction, superfluity, and so forth" (Kugel, "On the Bible and Literary Criticism," p. 223).

9. Ibid., p 234.

10. Northrop Frye, *The Great Code: The Bible and Literature* (New York: Harcourt Brace Jovanovich, 1982), p. 224. Hereafter referred to in the text as *TGC*.

11. Literary interests are not seen as doing an injustice to the religious concern with Jesus Christ, for the literature of the Bible itself "is our only real contact with the so-called 'Jesus of history'" (*TGC*, p. 77).

12. Michael Fishbane, "The Notion of a Sacred Text" (paper delivered at Conference on "Sacred Texts," Indiana University, October 17-20, 1982), pp. 15-17.

13. Ibid.

14. In deconstructionist terms, biblical texts write across and deconstruct other biblical texts. The reinterpretation by Micah of Isaiah's messianic hope is an example of this deconstruction. Fishbane sees this rewriting as a hint of the "transformative vision of 'concordant discord.' " Isaiah had envisioned an era of peace in which all nations were to go to Zion and be instructed by the God of Israel (Isaiah 2:1-4). Micah received this tradition but added one revolutionary coda: each nation (Israel included) would go in the name of its own God (Micah 4:5). Fishbane suggests that Micah "saw the multiple visions of peace of all peoples as converging synergistically towards a truth which Israel knows through its god. No symbolic construction would exclude any other: concordant discord" (Fishbane, "The Notion of a Sacred Text," pp. 17-18).

15. Ibid., p. 18.

16. Alan Richardson, "The Rise of Modern Biblical Scholarship and Recent Discussion of the Authority of the Bible," in *Cambridge History of the Bible*, vol. 3, "The West from the Reformation to the Present Day," ed. S. L. Greenslade (Cambridge, England: Cambridge University Press, 1963), p. 318.

17. Northrop Frye, *Anatomy of Criticism: Four Essays* (Princeton, N.J.: Princeton University Press, 1957), p. 162. Excerpts from this work copyright © 1957 by Princeton University Press. Used by permission. Hereafter referred to in the text as *AC*.

18. Sternberg sees the essential significance of the biblical plot as the expression of the move from ignorance to knowledge and the recapitulation of that movement in the life of the reader. Even if that is too limited a definition of the comic thrust, Sternberg's recognition that the basic movement is a result of ideology is valid.

19. See Leland Ryken, *How to Read the Bible as Literature* (Grand Rapids, Mich.: Academie Books), pp. 187-90, for a catalog of archetypes arranged on the basis of "ideal" and "unideal."

20. Robert Alter, *The Art of Biblical Narrative* (New York: Basic Books, 1981), p. 51. Alter sees evidence of such larger type-scenes in the "perplexing fact that in biblical narrative more or less the same story often seems to be told two or three or more times about different characters, or sometimes even about the same character in different sets of circumstances" (p. 49). Instead of explaining this fact by a theory of a duplication of sources, Alter proposes "a series of recurrent narrative episodes attached to the careers of biblical heroes that are analogous to Homeric type-scenes in that they are dependent on the manipulation of a fixed constellation of predetermined motifs" (p. 51).

21. See M. D. Goulder, *Type and History in Acts* (London: S.P.C.K., 1964).

22. Northrop Frye, *The Secular Scripture: A Study of the Structure of Romance*, The Charles Eliot Norton Lectures, 1974-75 (Cambridge, Mass.: Harvard University Press, 1976), pp. 15, 60.

23. Ibid., pp. 60-61.

24. Sternberg's view of the role of the Bible as involving the movement from ignorance to knowledge in the life of the reader as well as in the text is suggestive insofar as the creation of their world by men and women. The originality of the Bible's world view is seen as "the shift of ground from existence to epistemology." In the Bible, God stands opposed to humankind in terms of knowledge, and nowhere else in Oriental and Greek literature "does the variable of knowledge assume such a cutting edge and such a dominant role" (*PBN*, p. 46).

25. Fishbane, "The Notion of a Sacred Text," p. 20.

26. Ibid., pp. 20-21.

27. *The Death of God* is the title of a 1961 publication in which Gabriel Vahanian noted the fact that many twentieth-century people operate without belief in God. The Death of God theology attempted to accommodate Christian theology to this cultural fact.

28. The inadequacies of analogy actually resulted in the development of a nonverbal mystical tradition in which no word was seen as strictly applicable to God. Words are finite, and God is not finite.

29. Robert Alter points out that the biblical narratives are translations of "the basic perspective that man must live before God, in the transforming medium of time, incessantly and perplexingly in relation with others," and that "God's purposes are always entrammeled in history, dependent on the acts of individual men and women for their continuing realization" (Alter, *The Art of Biblical Narrative*, pp. 22, 12).

30. Shemaryahu Talmon, "The 'Comparative Method' in Biblical Interpretation—Principles and Problems," *Göttingen Congress Volume* (Leiden, 1978), p. 354. Meir Sternberg shows how the role of "reenactment" may be assigned to biblical narrative even though this is transformed because of the "historical" nature of the narrative. The biblical narrator "constructs a twofold rhetoric, extending to the implied reader the signs and message that God directs at his own refractory clients. God operates and comments to manifest his power in his proper sphere of activity; the narrator, in his guise as objective recorder, stages and preserves the divine manifestations for all time" (*PBN*, p. 103).

31. Some would emphasize a deconstructionist view of language and logic in which no stable meaning exists—much less a transcendent deity posited as the ground of such meaning. Jacques Derrida is the philosopher who is most frequently cited in support of the loss of any stable meaning, linguistically and philosophically. His seminal essay on "Différance" enunciated the differential nature of language and the continual deferring of meaning. In a playful way, Derrida utilized the fact that différance and *difference* are pronounced the same way in French (the essay was originally an address given before the *Sociètè française de philosophie*). Conceived of as resulting from the Latin *differre*, the terms would have two distinct meanings: to defer and to differ. The more common and identifiable sense of the French verb *différer* is to differ—"to be not identical, to be other, discernible, etc." The more opaque meaning (in French) is to defer—"*Différer* in this sense is to temporize, to take recourse, consciously or unconsciously, in the temporal and temporizing mediation of a detour that suspends the accomplishment or fulfillment of 'desire' or 'will,' and equally effects this suspension in a mode

that annuls or tempers its own effect" (Jacques Derrida, "Différance," in *Margins of Philosophy*, trans. Alan Bass [Chicago: University of Chicago Press, 1982], p. 8). In the address, Derrida utilizes Saussure's structuralist concept of language to establish the idea that "language, or any code, any system of referral in general, is constituted 'historically' as a weave of differences" (Derrida, "Différance," p. 12). This is not a result of the activity of the speaking subject; the speaking subject is itself a "function" of language. It is not the result of a "presence" prior to speech. "Thus one comes to posit presence—and specifically consciousness, the being beside itself of consciousness—no longer as the absolutely essential form of Being, but as a 'determination' and as an 'effect' " (Derrida, "Différance," pp. 16-17).

32. Frye cites Einstein's realization that instead of being "the great bastion of the objectivity of the world," matter is "an illusion of energy" (*TGC*, p. 14).

33. John Macquarrie, *Principles of Christian Theology* (New York: Charles Scribner's Sons, 1966), pp. 118-20.

34. Ibid., p. 115.

35. Ibid., p. 103.

36. Ibid., p. 116.

37. Ibid., p. 75.

38. Ibid., p. 79.

39. Ibid., p. 117.

40. Eugene Thomas Long, *Existence, Being and God: An Introduction to the Philosophical Theology of John Macquarrie* (New York: Paragon House Publishers, 1985), p. 54.

41. Ibid., p. 95.

Chapter Five

The Role of the Reader: Actualizing of Biblical Discourse

This chapter continues the discussion of the role of the reader begun in chapter 4, concentrating on specific strategies of actualization performed by readers and the actualization of the reader in the process. The reader begins with the words on the page, which may be thought of as the basic data to be read or processed initially on the basis of linguistic and literary codes. In the initial section of this chapter, the reader's activities in actualizing the verbal content of a biblical text are delineated. The second section discusses the role of the reader in determining a reference of the text or theme that will have contemporary significance. The third section emphasizes the actualization of the reader, which takes place in the process of reading.

Actualizing the Verbal Content of Biblical Texts

The synthesis of meaning at the level of what is being said—the verbal meaning—is generally a fairly easy procedure, which we carry out unaware of the way our minds operate in the process. The way a complete thought (a sentence) is created out of a collection of words may be taken as the pattern for reading in general. It is a matter of selecting the meanings of words and sentences that result in an appropriate overall coordination.

The Initial Actualization

If we picture reading as a left to right process (in keeping with the conventions of the English language), we see the beginning of the process as the entering of words, phrases, sentences, and series of sentences from the left-hand side. These language elements are processed initially in terms of the reader's knowledge and competence of lexical items and the grammar of the natural language.

The determination of the meanings of words is an art as well as a science, since any one word has a wider range of uses and meanings than can be accommodated in one sentence. The procedure followed by the reader in the actualization of potential meanings involves the disregarding of certain alternatives and the selecting of others on the basis of meanings previously established (contextual) and meanings established by external circumstances (circumstantial). Readers infer meanings on the basis of common frames (which comes from knowledge of particular texts) and intertextual frames (which comes from knowledge of biblical literature in general). A reader actualizes aspects of the potential offered by the words and phrases that cohere with decisions about the structure and meaning of the entire sentence. A reader entertains only a small number of possibilities for each word as the sentence is processed. A postulated topic serves as the filter for the selection of meaning possibilities of the words and phrases of the sentence, and the successful amalgamation validates the choice of topic.

For non-literary texts that refer directly and unambiguously to the real world, the grammar of the natural language and knowledge of the real world may suffice for making sense of the text. The world of the text and the world to which the text refers are the same, and the task is to achieve correspondence (in the case of truth) or to demonstrate lack of correspondence (in the case of error). For non-literary texts, a reader supposes circumstances of writing that support the decision to read the text as non-literary. When the textual content and grammar and syntax do not demand a revision of the supposition, the processing of the text is essentially a reduction of the content of the text to real-world data and categories. In making a decision, readers switch back and forth among different systems—that which is known or supposed about the circumstances of origin of the text, the text as it appears on the page with its lexical and grammatical constructions, the codes of the natural language, and the real world.

For literary texts, an appropriate "grammar" is also necessary (knowledge of the conventions peculiar to literature and peculiar to the particular type of literary text being read). Since the worlds of literary texts are extensions of real worlds, however, knowledge of the real world is also necessary for processing literary texts. The narratives of the patriarchs and of Jesus and his disciples, for example, are not appropriately processed simply by establishing correspondence between the worlds of those narratives and the actual worlds of the patriarchs and Jesus (as far as they can be known). Textual content and structures of biblical narrative go far beyond the reach of the grammar of the natural language. Since the narrative world is not unrelated to the real world, however, the imaging of the narrative world by the writer and by the reader is not totally discontinuous with the real world.

As a reader processes a text, he or she will use all of the data and systems necessary to make sense of the portion of text being processed. Right-hand schemata (categories of structure and content) will be somewhat automatically developed which are adequate for the left-hand structure and content. Letters of the alphabet, for example, are processed with the expectation that they will form words. Letters are not perceived as independent units but as potential for words. Letters seek to be perceived as words. Words, on the other hand, anticipate letters, which are necessary to complete their structure and meaning. Paralleling the word processing is sentence processing at both the syntactic and the semantic levels. Words seek to be perceived as sentences, and sentences seek words to complete the sort of form and content anticipated. But sentences fit into larger literary units, so sentences are fit together to form stories, letters, sermons, and other categories. Readers will move from the linear text manifestation to whatever system is necessary in order to make sense of the unit being processed.

The text is actualized in such a fashion that it will have modern-day relevance, so the system of the reader's world is important. But since the contemporary relevance is mediated and not direct, the reader cannot ignore the ancient circumstances of the text's origin. The reader should not attempt to visualize the writers as intending (in a narrow sense) to communicate with contemporary readers in their particular situations. In the process of reading, then, a reader will move back and forth from the text as source and ancient discourse and the text as contemporary discourse. The words on the page are put into play both by the reader's determination of circumstances of the origin of the text and by the reader's direction of the text to serve as contemporary communication. The moves made by the reader are somewhat intuitive and involve at some time or another all of the linguistic and literary codes known by the reader, the circumstances of origin of the text, and the real world, with its different systems (historical, sociological, psychological, economic, ideological, and so on).

A General Point of View: Artistry or Facticity? We come to a biblical text and must decide in a preliminary way—consciously or unconsciously—how to read it. Rules or conventions of overcoding tell a reader if codes beyond the natural language are to be applied. Overcoding is the application of a new rule on the basis of and in addition to the rule of the natural language. It involves single words, phrases, and entire literary works (figures of speech and genre on various levels, for example).

> A basic code establishes that a certain grammatical disposition is understandable and acceptable (how and why) and a further rule (which, far from denying the previous one, assumes it as a starting point) establishes that the disposition in question has to be used under

given circumstances and with a certain stylistic connotation (for example, "epic style" or "poetic dignity").[1]

"Once upon a time" is an overcoded expression. An incompetent reader could apply only the rules of the natural language and take it as a definite temporal designation. But competent readers know that the events to be related following the expression are not "real" and that they "take place" in an indefinite nonhistorical epoch. The reader is reading fiction.

"In the beginning" has been taken as a definite temporal designation, and the application of the code of the natural language alone has led to all sorts of misunderstandings. Arguments have taken place over whether the reference is absolute or whether matter already existed when God created. The stories that follow have been understood as attempts to describe historical events (not only the narratives of the patriarchs with their stories of strife between brothers, parental preference, barren wives, and so on, but also stories of Adam and Eve, the speaking serpent, and the flood). The attempt in the seventeenth century to fix the date for the creation of the world (4004 B.C.) is a natural result of failure to see the overcoding involved in Genesis. So powerful is the assumption that the Bible is not subject to literary codes built upon the code of the natural language that a committee of a large denomination recently declared that "the narratives of Scripture are historically and factually accurate."[2] These narratives include the opening chapters of Genesis. Genesis, therefore, teaches that creation of humankind took place directly and that Adam and

Eve were real persons. The president of the denomination (who served on the committee) later modified the impact of the report by declaring that the statement did not rule out figurative use of language within the Bible.

The sophisticated reduction of the Bible to sources by historical criticism has led to scholarly limitations of the potential of biblical texts. But the same principle is involved. To read the biblical text as source is to read it as the container of some sort of information that may be extracted by objective procedures and validated by comparing the data obtained with data in the real world. To read the biblical text as ancient communication does not really alter the model. The data emphasized is the sort that gives attention to the ancient situation of communication. The rhetorical artistry involved is subordinated to facticity.

To *begin* with the view of the Bible as source in some sense and to subject it to scientific codes makes movement beyond these sorts of critical meanings problematic. To read the Bible as literature is to retrieve it from the museum, to relate it to the life of contemporary readers. The reader of the Bible as literature will begin not by directing it to something outside but by giving attention to the relationships within the text, the relationship of words to sentences and of sentences to larger literary units.

The Reader and Ambiguity. Readers assume that a text makes sense as a linguistic and literary unit and intuitively use their linguistic and literary competence in the process of actualization. When ambiguity arises, a reader becomes conscious of the process that is being followed. When we read in II Samuel 13 that David's son Absalom has his brother Amnon killed, we are able to make sense of the text. We know the appropriate categories and are able to work out the logic of cause-and-effect, since we know from earlier information that Absalom is avenging Amnon's rape of Tamar, their sister. But when we read, "And David mourned for his son day after day" (II Samuel 13:37), we have a problem. Is it for the murdered Amnon that David mourns or for the murderer, Absalom, who has been forced to flee to Geshur? What sense is a reader to make? What categories are appropriate?

In the processing of the text, then, the reader will discover that the text (intentionally and unintentionally) does not (indeed, *cannot*) make explicit all that must be known to make sense of the text. Grammatical and syntactical structures and semantic information must be identified and supplied in order for the text to fit the codes and conventions. In the process, moreover, the codes and conventions with which the reader begins may be modified.

Grammatical structures of biblical Hebrew and Greek, no less than their English equivalents, are often ambiguous. Abraham replies, "God will provide for Himself the lamb for the burnt offering, my son" (Genesis 22:8 NASB) at the time Isaac questions him about the absence of an offering. Is the "my son" to be understood as the vocative or as an apposition? Is Abraham here indicating that Isaac is the offering provided by God? "Let not your heart be troubled; believe in God, believe also in me" (John 14:1 NASB) is ambiguous because the second person plural indicative and imperative forms are identical. Is the Jesus of John's Gospel acknowledging belief in God and in himself (both indicative) on the part of his hearers, pleading for belief in God and himself (both imperative), or acknowledging belief in God and using that as a basis for a plea for faith in himself? When Paul says that God "chose to reveal his Son *in* me" (Galatians 1:16), does he mean "to me," "through me," "in my heart," or "in my case"? The dative case is capable of indicating any of these relationships. Is "the love of God" (Luke 11:42; Romans 5:5; II Corinthians 13:14) God's love directed toward others, love directed toward God, or both? Is the "faith of Jesus Christ" (Romans 3:22; Galatians 2:16; 3:22; Philippians 3:9; and Ephesians 3:12) faith directed toward Jesus Christ or the faith Jesus has in God? Does the "first fruits of the Spirit" (Romans 8:23) refer to the Spirit as the first installment of a more abundant harvest to come or to a first installment that comes from the Spirit? The reader must make inferences or clarify presuppositions to deal with grammatical and syntactical ambiguity. Some inferences are textual; from a preceding part of the text, or in some instances from what follows, the reference can be made specific. At times, decision must be made from what we know of the tradition of the text, from other texts, from the totality of the world presupposed by the text, or from the real world.

The presence of *pro-type words* (such as pronouns and adverbs) is related to the problem of ambiguity and the need for inference. Such words must be transformed in the consciousness of the reader to the original reference (person, place, time, and so on). In John 7:38 ("out of *his* heart shall flow rivers of living water"), is the reference to the heart of Jesus or to the heart of believers? In Genesis 34:31, the brothers of Joseph question, "Shall *he* treat our sister as a harlot?" This question arises after Dinah's seduction by Shechem, her brothers' painful retribution, and Jacob's chastisement of the brothers. Are the brothers talking about the treatment of their sister as a harlot by Shechem or by Jacob? Does the "now" in Ephesians 3:5 (the mystery "which was not made known to the sons of men in other generations . . . has *now* been revealed to his holy apostles and prophets") refer to some recent experience of revelation of the share Gentiles have in Christ, or does it refer to the time of the Christian era in distinction from the period before Christ?

Normally, the ambiguity involved in the subordinate grammatical and syntactical structures can be handled by the reader because one actualization fits the total linguistic and literary context better than others. When different actualizations fit the same context equally well, the reader may process the text in the different ways allowed by the ambiguity.

Poetic Omission. Deliberate omission of words is often a reflection of creative or poetic languages. Poetic omission not only makes the text more striking, but it also involves the reader in completing the text. The omission of verbs in the following examples is relatively easy to fill in by the reader.

> Out of Zion shall go forth the law, and the word of the Lord from Jerusalem. (Isaiah 2:3 KJV)
>
> And all the people saw the thunderings, and the lightnings, and the noise of the trumpet, and the mountain smoking. (Exodus 20:18 KJV)

In each case, the missing verb is found in an earlier clause. The case of "seeing" the noise of the thunder, of course, requires the reader's imagination.

In many cases, the reader must supply needed material without assistance from the immediate context. From the larger context, the postulated topic, knowledge of the cultural and religious backgrounds , and personal experience, the reader supplies what is needed. The following passages illustrate the necessity for the reader to supply not only conjunctions and verbs but also nouns and whole prepositional phrases.

> God judgeth the righteous, and God is angry with the wicked every day. (Psalm 7:11 KJV)
>
> For a day in thy courts is better than a thousand. I had rather be a doorkeeper in the house of my God, than to dwell in the tents of wickedness. (Psalm 84:10 KJV)
>
> Mine age is departed, and is removed from me as a shepherd's tent: I have cut off like a weaver my life. (Isaiah 38:12 KJV)

The translators of the King James Version make sense of Psalm 7:11 by the insertion of "the wicked" in the second line: "God judgeth the righteous, and God is angry *with the wicked* every day." Isaiah 38:12 requires some knowledge of the work of the weaver in order to complete the thought: "I have cut off my life as a weaver cuts off his threads."

Paratactic Thinking. Paratactic constructions abound in biblical Hebrew and Greek and may be taken as the paradigm for reader-oriented biblical poetics. (The illustrations above contain paratactic constructions as well as poetic omissions.) In parataxis, two ideas are set side by side without the relationship between them being specified. Readers must supply information in order to adjudicate the relationship. A literal translation would render Genesis 24:56: "Do not detain me *and* the Lord has made my journey successful." Jeremiah 4:10 would read, "You have said, 'You shall have peace, *and* the sword is at your throats.' " And Mark 15:25 would be: "It was nine o'clock *and* they crucified him." A reader must detect whether the relationship is causal, conditional, circumstantial, concessive, final, and so on.

The decipherment of the psalmist's hymn on the eloquence of the heavenly bodies requires more than a determination of the circumstances involved.

> They have no speech or language,
>   their voice is not heard;
> Their music goes out through all the earth,
>   their words reach to the end of the world.
> (Psalm 19:3-4)

The contrast between the first two lines and the last two is absolute! George Caird suggests that Joseph Addison's following eight lines reflecting the Age of Reason is an appropriate match for what the psalmist is expressing.[3]

> What though in solemn silence all
> Move round the dark terrestrial ball?
> What though no real voice nor sound
> Amid their radiant orbs be found?
> In reason's ear they all rejoice,
> And utter forth a glorious voice,
> For ever singing, as they shine,
> "The hand that made us is divine."

Not all biblical scholars have been so perceptive. The Septuagint translator apparently thought the contradiction between the first and last two lines was too great for mediation. He translated the first two lines:

> There is no speech or language
> Where their voice is not heard.

This translation has found its way into the King James Version through the Vulgate.[4]

The assumption of the Septuagint translator was that the Bible could not give such discomfort and require readers to accommodate simultaneous silence and speech. Recent studies in biblical poetry, however, disagree with the comfortable assumption. The indefiniteness of the relationship and the necessity of finding the precise connection are seen by James L. Kugel as "the whole point" of juxtaposed clauses, especially in proverbs and sayings.[5] This task of discovery is related to the quality of "sharpness" most often associated with Hebrew proverbs—where juxtaposing is most common. Ecclesiastes 12:11 associates the proverb with something sharp: "The sayings of the wise are sharp as goads, like nails driven home; they lead the assembled people" (NEB). The proverb is sharp, however, not because it "spurred to action or pricked the conscience of the listener." This meaning is an adaptation of a primary attribute already known and associated with riddles, the testing of wits, and verbal showmanship. The sharpness of the proverb is "the delight in creating a B half which both connects with, and yet cleverly expands, the meaning of A. 'Sharpness' represented the potential subtleties hidden inside juxtaposed clauses." The delight in decipherment offered by hidden subtleties is "the genius of the form."[6]

Paratactic composition requiring the reader's completion goes beyond even complicated linguistic constructions. Biblical paradox in general may be included here. In the eleventh chapter of Hebrews, for example, the author says that those who in the past have lived by faith "saw God's promises fulfilled" (11:33) and yet "did not obtain the promise" (11:39). The reader is obliged to draw the proper relationship between these two ideas.[7] This activity of the reader is one of the ways that Hebrews achieves its reader-oriented function.

With the objects of concern ranging from simple linguistic parallels to the parallels of an idea in a literary unit and what that unit facilitates in the imagination of the reader, or even to paradox, a reader of the Bible has to recapitulate the ability of the author to "think paratactically."[8]

Identification of Figures. With figures or metaphors that can be classified as instances of substitution or comparison, the reader simply substitutes the literal meaning for figurative expressions. In such cases, a reader must determine whether the literal meaning makes sense. If not, another meaning is substituted. *Interactive metaphors* go beyond such substitution and require a sort of paratactic thinking. Interactive metaphors foster insight into both sides of the comparison and involve the reader's wit more fully than does a simple substitution.

> Their mode of operation requires the reader to use a system of implications (a system of "commonplaces"—or a special system established for the purpose in hand) as a means for selecting, emphasizing, and organizing relations in a different field. This use of a "subsidiary subject" to foster insight into a "principal subject" is a distinctive *intellectual* operation (though one familiar enough through our experience of learning anything whatever), demanding simultaneous awareness of both subjects but not reducible to any *comparison* between the two.[9]

Contemporary study of Jesus' parables of the kingdom benefits from "paratactic thinking," which does not reduce the parable as metaphor to some predetermined concept of kingdom but allows the parables of the kingdom and the kingdom so figured to interact in a way that new knowledge and insight result.[10]

Temporal and Logical Discontinuity. Temporal and logical discontinuity must be handled by the reader by an inference of relationships from what has transpired or will later transpire in the text, from other texts, from the world of the text, or from the real world. The narrative of Judges 14:1-4 illustrates the need for inference, which is supplied by later information.

> Samson went down to Timnah, and at Timnah he saw one of the daughters of the Philistines. Then he came up, and told his father and mother, "I saw one of the daughters of the Philistines at Timnah; now get her for me as my wife." But his father and mother said to him, "Is there not a woman among the daughters of your kinsmen, or among all our people, that you must go to

take a wife from the uncircumcised Philistines?" But Samson said to his father, "Get her for me; for she pleases me well."

His father and mother did not know that it was from the Lord; for he was seeking an occasion against the Philistines. At that time the Philistines had domination over Israel. (Judges 14:1-4)

It is not only the parents of Samson who wonder why their son plans to marry a Philistine. Readers want to know why a deliverer of Israel wants to enter into a marriage with a member of the nation oppressing his people. Readers may supply appropriate motivation from their own experience of living and reading, but when we come to the end of the brief narrative, we discover the canonical motivation and order of occurrence: God was intent on delivering Israel from its oppressors and sought to make trouble between Samson and the Philistines by Samson's marriage with a Philistine woman.

The temporal discontinuity and the process the reader follows in reordering and making sense of this short narrative is a pattern for more lengthy narratives and even entire books of the Bible. The brief lapse between the reader's questioning of Samson's motive and the supplying of the answer may hide the significance of the reader's activity in such narratives. In the story of Gideon (Judges 6:1–8:35), however, the reader must wait for three chapters for satisfaction of curiosity concerning Gideon's reason for extraordinary perseverance and blood thirstiness in pursuing Zebah and Zalmunna, the kings of Midian. In the process of reading three chapters, the reader no doubt attributes Gideon's action to religious devotion. It is only in 8:18-19 that we discover that Zebah and Zalmunna had slain Gideon's brothers, and we are able to infer that personal revenge is a part of Gideon's motivation. Prosaic readers may take the temporal discontinuity in the case of the story of Gideon (and other stories) to be the result of an incompetent author or an accident in transmission. A note in the *Oxford Annotated Bible*, for example, suggests that "the original beginning of the story must have recorded the death of Gideon's brothers at the hands of the Midianites and his resolve, as their next of kin, to avenge them."[11]

The reader must read the entire book of Jonah to discover why Jonah goes to such great lengths to avoid going to Nineveh to preach, and no theory of transmission error can delude us into thinking that this is not intentional. Inquisitive readers (the readers intended by the book of Jonah) will not wait until the end, however. They will wonder if Jonah is too tenderhearted to preach the message of doom to the great city or if Jonah is protesting the wrath of God.

It is only at the very end of the story that we get the answer.

> When God saw what they did, how they turned from their evil way, God repented of the evil which he had said he would do to them; and he did not do it. But it displeased Jonah exceedingly, and he was angry. And he prayed to the Lord and said, "I pray thee, Lord, is not this what I said when I was yet in my country? That is why I made haste to flee to Tarshish; for I knew that thou art a gracious God and merciful, slow to anger, and

abounding in steadfast love, and repentest of evil. (Jonah 3:10–4:2)

Coherence as the Key to Reading. Coherence is the key to the determination of indeterminate grammatical and syntactical structures, the solution of problems of ambiguity, and the establishment of motivation and order in the text. But this is a key to reading even if ambiguity and disorder are not present. This key demands the reader's involvement at every level. Topics or schemata on various levels—sentences, short sequences, and entire texts—provide a basis for coherence. Just as a word has potential for a variety of meanings, however, a text has potentiality for more than one topic. The linear text manifestation is the result of the co-existence of many codes or sub-codes and functions on the basis of multiple imbedded topics. For the reader who is aware of the varied and intertwined nature of the text and the plurality of topics, the determination of a topic is a result of more than intellectual deduction. The will of the reader as well as the intellect is involved in this determination.[12]

From a particular psychological "set," from key words in the text, and from other apparent or hidden regularities, the reader presupposes a topic that might cause the entire text to make sense. The reader then moves from this supposition or guess as to the topic back to the components of the text to see if a coherence results. The topic then directs the amalgamation and organization of a level of sense. The reader need not consider consciously all of the syntactic and semantic possibilities in movement from words to more ultimate levels of meaning, only those that make sense within the chosen framework.

One strategy that may be used to enable the move to an initial understanding of what is happening in a short text, on the basis of the linear level of manifestation, is the reduction or transformation of the linear level into a series of active sentences with the subjects and objects expressed as nouns and not as pronouns and with implicit information (inferences and assumptions) made explicit. The text will be ordered logically as well as grammatically. With this assignment, the reader will use linguistic and literary capacity in an unconscious way to understand what is going on in the text and to make this knowledge explicit. Where inferences are necessary, the reader will infer. Where a literal verbal meaning does not "make sense," the reader will supply appropriate figurative meaning. Semantic properties of verbs and syntactic operations will be actualized and performed to cause the text as a whole to make sense. The result of the process is a synthesis made by the reader. It is an actualization of the discursive structures of the text. It must be remembered, however, that this actualization cannot be equated with the text. Other actualizations are possible.

Progressive Actualization, Retrospection, and Multiple Actualizations

The procedure described to this point is only part of what happens with the reading of literary texts.

The process is made more complicated by such things as the segment by segment processing of lengthy texts, the influence of rereading on the entire process, and the possibility of different and multiple actualizations of the entire text.

Progressive Actualization. The linear unfolding of the text and the result of the progressive actualization of the text must be given serious attention from a reader-oriented perspective. A reader makes sense of one segment in something of the way described earlier, and then the reader confronts another segment. What is the relationship between the first segment and the succeeding segments? The text itself does not fill in the connections. The reader must progressively fill in the gaps or blanks and thereby form the segments of the text. In doing this, the reader creates a framework within which the two segments can be grasped as a unified pattern. In the process, a reader focuses on one segment, which is the "theme." Once this segment has been actualized, the reader moves to the next segment, which becomes a new "theme." The other segment, however, remains as the horizon against which the new segment is actualized.[13] The same sort of paratactic thinking is involved as in poetry, with the exception that a cumulative series is involved.

John 7:1-9 tells of Jesus' going about in Galilee instead of Judea because of danger in Jerusalem. When his brothers encourage him to "leave here and go to Judea, that your disciples may see the works you are doing" (v. 3), Jesus responds, "Go to the feast yourselves; I am not going up to this feast" (v. 8). In the very next segment, however, the text indicates: "But after his brothers had gone up to the feast, then he also went up, not publicly but in private" (John 7:10). A reader will make sense of the first segment in the easiest way possible: Jesus is not going to Jerusalem to celebrate the feast. The next segment forces a complete reevaluation of what the reader considered the only possible reading of the initial segment.

The reader's activity in making sense of the series of segments is related to activity in making sense of the entire text. The literary text offers a perspective, or a view, of the world through a system of perspectives that shade into one another and converge on a "general meeting place." This convergence (which can be called "the meaning of the text") is not actually stated or represented in the literary text. It is left unstated, just as is the relationship between lines of poetry or between the segments of narrative. The convergence or meaning depends on the standpoint that is lacking in the text. The reader is provided potential by the text, but the reader must determine or actualize meaning. The reader's role is structured by the perspectives given in the text, the vantage point from which the reader draws the perspectives of the text, and the converging point. Different ways of fulfilling the process are allowed, however, because of the dynamics of the process. "The process of fulfillment is always a selective one, and any one actualization can be judged against the background of the others potentially present in the textual structure of the reader's role."[14]

The Gospel of Mark presents peculiar difficulties in the segment by segment processing, which may be related to the convergence of perspectives into a "general meeting place." Readers who have been influenced by the form-critical attention to the individual units may attempt to escape the ambitious task of relating the series of actions in 1:4–3:35 to one another. The conclusion of the story of Jesus' healing on the Sabbath ("The Pharisees went out, and immediately held counsel with the Herodians against him, how to destroy him"), however, encourages the reader to organize the segments into a story that will conclude with the passion. The early stories of Jesus' success in chapters 1–3 serve as motivation for the plot of his enemies against Jesus, recounted at the beginning of chapter 3. The chapter on parables (ch. 4), with its emphasis on the "secret" of the kingdom of God, relativizes such a passion-directed processing. The reader may even despair of making any sense of the materials as a whole. Later on in the Gospel, moreover, the reader is encouraged once again to tie segments together as the author specifies relationships. In Mark 8:19, the Jesus of the Gospel of Mark questions the disciples about events recorded earlier in the Gospel: " 'When I broke the five loaves for the five thousand, how many baskets full of broken pieces did you take up?' They said to him, 'Twelve.' 'And the seven for the four thousand, how many baskets full of broken pieces did you take up?' And they said to him, 'Seven.' And he said to them, 'Do you not yet understand?' " (Mark 8:19-21).

The reader may be inclined at that point to think that the "general meeting place" and meaning of Mark have been achieved with the theme of understanding. The reader's inclination is supported by his or her superior understanding. This, however, provides the basis for dramatic irony, which may suggest an altogether different "meeting place" for the themes of the various segments.

Retrospection. The theme and horizon view of reading influences the forward movement, but it also involves a backward movement. Retrospection, as well as anticipation, is involved in the reading process. One statement opens up a horizon that is modified or even completely changed by following statements. A new actualization of earlier material takes place as new significance is seen.[15]

The story of Samson's infatuation with the Philistine woman illustrates the need both to reshape the sequence and to reevaluate the meaning and significance, as there is a shift in level and plan from human to divine. The concluding verses of Jonah shatter expectations so completely that the reader may become disoriented.

> Hardly has he recovered from the surprise of God's repentance, contrary to all expectations about the future, when he discovers his reading of the past turned upside down. Not that the plot and the participants are suddenly transformed, but that they are suddenly recognized for what they have always been; and if they look transformed, that is only because the narrator has passed in misleading silence over what the prophet actually said "when [he] was yet in [his] own country" in response to God's original command. (*PBN*, pp. 319-20)

Multiple Actualizations. In the reading and actualization of a text, a particular topic, theme, or idea presents itself or is imposed by the reader. As long as the textual data do not require a radical change of perspective, a reader will move to the end of the story, utilizing the textual data to fill out that topic or idea. Materials that could be used for the development of additional ideas are put into a subsidiary relationship with the main theme. The Gospel of Mark has been observed as an example of writing that encourages different themes, which are not necessarily incompatible. In some cases, however, alternate readings may not be compatible. Why does Uriah "not go down to his house" (II Samuel 11:9) after David has brought him home from war? Does Uriah know about his wife's affair with David? The text never allows an unequivocal answer. The gap may be filled legitimately by both affirmative and negative answers. Each hypothesis is supported by a good number of arguments, but other arguments indicate its flaws and support the opposite answer. This situation is deliberate. The text demands that both hypotheses be utilized to shed their different light on details in the text; different plots must be organized on the basis of the hypotheses. Moreover, the text requires the reader to maintain both hypotheses simultaneously. The text and the reader profit from such an interaction. (See *PBN*, pp. 201-2.)

The composition of the Uriah story has been seen as forming a "basic principle of the literary text and a key to biblical ambiguity" (*PBN*, p. 202).

> The coexistence of two (or more) mutually exclusive hypotheses—concerning action, motive, character—always enables the author to kill two birds with one stone, using the same materials for different ends. Above all, it

enables him to base sequence and effect on the tensions between the two possibilities. Each reading may serve to balance and ironize the other. The emergence of such a hypothesis in a text that equally validates its contrary renders each quite unlike a similar hypothesis appearing unchallenged. A simultaneous reading of a text from two unresolvable perspectives, with its constant movement between the rivals, not only enriches every doubled construct, actional or psychological. It inevitably makes for heightened perceptibility. It sharpens our awareness of the work's verbal art, foregrounds the modes of expression, and brings out the more subtle features of the represented events. Each detail assumes importance, deriving from the support or resistance it offers to the hypotheses and from the coincident pleasure afforded by its double reading. In short, the ambiguity calls attention to the literary texture as such. (*PBN*, p. 228)

Readers who wish to make sense of biblical texts may not give uncritical allegiance to some radical deconstructive views, but they can benefit from contemporary emphasis on the fact that no particular context, no particular theme or topic, allows saturation of all the data of a text. The meaning of a text is inexhaustible because no context can provide all the keys to all of its possibilities.

Actualizing the Reference of Biblical Texts

In chapter 4, the Bible was discussed as a means of humanizing readers through its "revelation" of the sacred, and suggestions were made for the reader's contemporary imaging of the sacred. To this point in the present chapter, we have emphasized the reader's actualization of the text by means of linguistic and literary codes, lexicon, and the real world, and we have observed the potential of the text for the reader's creative activity of actualization. Between these two ideas—the imaging of the sacred and the actualization of the verbal structures of the text—stand matters such as genre, the reference of the actualized text, and interpretation. The perspective of a reader-oriented approach to biblical texts on these matters is somewhat different from conventional approaches in that the reader's role in situating the text (in terms of genre, theme, and interpretation) is vital for the accomplishment of the Bible's role and function.

Genre

The question of genre, from the prospective of reader-oriented literary studies, is not an optional question. Every reader reads a text in the light of its presumed nature as art or reality, poetry or prose, story or history, occasional letter or formal epistle, apocalypse or anti-apocalypse, and so on. When no conscious decision is made as to genre, a reader will read a text in accordance with conventions absorbed from religious, academic, and/or literary traditions or in accordance with the context of reading.

The question of genre could be a literary question returning us to source oriented approaches. Conventionally, the idea of genre has involved the denoting of important characteristics within a group of writings and the acceptance of those characteristics as defining a specific form of writing. The study of genre has also involved the analysis of the history related to the origins and developments of the forms.

The question of genre from a hermeneutic or reader-oriented perspective requires movement beyond the somewhat technical study of superficial correspondences between types of writings. Even so, the important results of historical genre study remain a valuable starting point. The fact that certain biblical writings can be classified as letters, for example, is helpful even though that classification is soon seen to be capable of further divisions, and eventually each letter is seen as occupying a unique place in the broad category. The question of the genre of the Gospels is intriguing as a historical question. Are the Gospels Hellenistic biographies? Is the Gospel form a recapitulation at a broader level of the pronouncement story (the form consisting of a short narrative with a concluding word of Jesus—termed *apothegm* by Bultmann)? Is the form something dramatically new in the history of the church? The reader cannot be neutral. The act of reading implies a decision as to whether the Gospels are history, realistic narrative, historical novel, sermon, or a combination. In fact, a reader has to come to some tentative hypothesis because he or she will begin to read the Gospel according to some conventions. That hypothesis and those conventions will be tested and made more precise in the process of reading. But whatever the hypothesis, the Gospel text itself will withstand attempts to exhaust its potential or submerge it completely within that hypothesis. The text will create its own conventions of reading.

In a reader centered approach, the conventions of genre are approached from the perspective of reading.[16] In a real sense, every writing is a unique genre in that every writing not only shares characteristics with *groups* of other writings, but it also maintains peculiar characteristics. In reading, a reader comes to appreciate the uniqueness of the particular writing, to see the writing as its own genre. Readers must not only respond to the demands of genre, but they also must actualize the genre as they actualize the literary work. A determination of genre, then, is a determination in the act of reading of how the text is to be read.

The Reader's Determination of Theme

In the actualization of biblical texts (as other literary texts) it is necessary for the reader to discern or formulate some theme or idea that serves as the basis for the reading process. The reading of any text can be directed to different points of view and levels of specificity. The whole of *Oedipus Rex* can be expressed as "find out the guilty!" But rather than the story of detection, it can be seen as the story of incest or parricide. Historical-critical approaches specify a point of view and a level of specificity that will illuminate most directly and explicitly the context of the origins of the text—the religious ideas of the ancient authors and their communities, historical and social events, relationships, and so on. The assumption is that the text is the result of historical causes and is to be understood and interpreted in terms of those causes. When discourse oriented concerns are coordinated with a view of the text as source, a "sender" and a "receiver" are identified or postulated, and the text is seen as an "object" directed from the "sender" to the "receiver." The textual object is defined in terms of the "intention" of the author in this communicaion. There is a coordination of the hypothetical situation of communication, the text as object, and the intention of the author.

If a biblical text is not directed toward facts related to its original context, what is the reality to which the text is directed? A reader-oriented approach will specify perspectives and levels that will illuminate the context of the reader. The narrative material can obviously be directed to the reality of the events depicted, to the reality of the author recounting the events, and/or to the original community for which the events were narrated. Can these historical levels of specification be transcended? Once it is observed that biblical narratives are not objective chronicles of events, the most natural move is to read them as literature.

As literature, attention is given to intratextual relations. A narrative is a linear unfolding of events from a beginning to an end. Readers make sense of the narrative by giving attention to the setting, the characters, and the plot. Events in the narrative move—often circuitously—toward resolution of some conflict, and readers are able to characterize the story on the basis of the sort of conflict (physical, emotional, moral, spiritual, and so on). Characters and actions are involved in the process toward resolution of the conflict, and readers relate the nature of the conflict and the episodic progress of the story to the types of characters performing the actions. The reader is able to discern meaning through the variety of intratextual relationships. But about what is the narrative speaking? As literature, different levels of reference are possible. James Kugel suggests some alternatives faced by the reader of the Joseph narrative. Is the narrative to be read as just another story? Or as a story with the premise "Let me tell you what happened to Joseph-your-ancestor?" Or, "Let me tell you how things came to be as you know them actually to be?" Or "Let me tell you how God has saved us?" Or "Let me tell you God's teachings?"[17]

Narrative materials of the Bible are most easily read as literary art with levels of reference related to the reader. However, didactic materials, such as letters, require special care to avoid reduction of the text to ancient communication. At the obvious surface level, the letter cannot be contemporary communication, for the reader does not stand in relation to the text as did the original readers. The reader of Paul's Letter to the Galatians, for example, does not share the relationship the original readers had with Paul and cannot read Galatians as a personal address in the original sense; for only a *brief* period did the text exist as personal address. It may be read as a historical document addressed to the ancient Galatian churches, dealing with their historically limited problem. (When read that way, historical answers will result. In itself, historical reading is not the most compelling sort of reading.) It may be read as addressed to the Christian community in general, dealing with the problem of Jewish law and Christian faith. (The Christian community imperceptibly made some such change as they continued to read the letter. This sort of reading is related to the canonical criticism emphasized by Brevard Childs.) Can we not read Galatians as addressed to believers of all persuasions, who must reconcile the old and the new? Or to humankind in general, who face the challenge and threat of freedom? (It must be remembered that the reading of Galatians in the light of a human concern, transcending time and parochial interests, is set in yet broader frameworks and functions of biblical texts.)

This approach does not deny that what the text is saying fits an ancient situation of communication within which the verbal meaning takes on significance. But it is possible to look beyond the historical particularities to seek the value that is being defended in the text in particular and even in provincial terms. With such an approach, the particular historically constrained character of the intention of the author and the topic does not relegate the meaning and significance to the past. The historically constrained particulars serve to illustrate and to highlight the more inclusive and reader-relevant theme. A literary approach to the Bible, rather than meaning the end of the Bible's use as a religious document, can mean the continued use of the Bible in and beyond the church.

The proposal for finding some satisfying idea beyond historical particularities is not a proposal to state the theme as some ontological truth and then to see the text as an illustration of such a truth. This would be another propositional approach, which would by-pass literary meaning and function in an attempt to transform the text to philosophy or theology. It is, however, a proposal to move away from a narrowly conceived "intention" of the author, constrained by a particular concrete situation.

The concept of the author's intention in literary studies, however, may be helpful in our project. The intention of the author has been used in literature to guard against undue subjectivity in interpretation. Biblical scholars who are interested in a hermeneutic approach to the Bible as literature and history-oriented scholars sometimes equate intentionality with narrow pragmatic purposes and uses. Literary scholars, however, do not speak of the author's intention in terms of the limited meaning of which an author is conscious or the meaning that is explicitly expressed in the text.

E. D. Hirsch compares author's meaning or intention with an iceberg. Only a part of the iceberg is present to sight, the smaller part. Even though the smaller part guides the examiner, the iceberg (and meaning) cannot be limited to that obvious part. What an author wills to convey is a "type," not a particular that makes sense *only* in terms of that particular. A type is an ideal that is able to represent and to embrace a variety of particulars.[18] In his early work, Hirsch spoke of the range of meaning possible in terms of *langue* (the language system, as opposed to *parole,* the actual concrete act of speaking by an individual).[19] This indicates the breadth of the range of meaning as well as the constraints of meaning.[20] The concept of author's intention may be a device to allow readers to state biblical themes and meanings in ways that allow them to remain faithful to and to relativize the particularities involved. Paul's Letter to the Romans may serve as an example. Attention may be given in Romans to Paul's own specific historical and psychological circumstances. Paul's message of justification may be seen as a "fighting doctrine" in the context of Paul's struggle against Jewish nomism. Romans, however, may be read in such a way that Jewish nomism (as understood and explicated by Paul in Romans) is simply one expression of "the community of 'good' people which turns God's promises into their own privileges and God's commandments into the instruments of self-sanctification."[21]

When readers change their backward source oriented approach to Romans to one oriented to the reader, they discover justification and resources for such an approach within the letter itself, for Paul's vision extended beyond the particular historical situation. Brevard S. Childs declares that, although Paul's letter is "addressed to a historically circumscribed, concrete church at Rome, in the course of his discourse this original addressee is altered in a variety of different ways."[22] The addressee and the argument assume representative and universal form in the letter itself. When Paul turns to deal with his Jewish protagonist in chapter 2 (following the conventions of the diatribe), the addressee becomes representative of all humanity, "Therefore, you have no excuse, O man, whoever you are." The "clearest use of representative language" is the move from the one to the many in the Adam figure of Romans 5, "For as by one man's disobedience many were made sinners, so by one man's obedience many will be made righteous" (5:19). The reader may be drawn into a direct confrontation as the movement is made from the one to the many. The profiling of a representative addressee in Romans 7 by use of the first person idiom is well known, but it is not limited to that famous passage. At the end of chapter 4, Paul moves from the third person to the inclusive "we," and in chapter 6 Paul appeals to the common experience of all Christians: "Do you not know that all of us who have been baptised into Christ Jesus were baptised into his death?" In chapters 14–15, the concrete character of Paul's addressee "recedes within the larger context and a universal referent emerges which far transcends local Roman party rivalries in order to speak a word for all."[23]

In the course of defending the position that God has maintained his promises to Israel in chapters 9–11, Paul demonstrates that the issue is not limited to some Jewish audience, theoretical though it be. The issue "involves God's universal salvation and . . . the existence of the church is dependent upon Israel's future . . . Paul's argument transcends completely the issue of regional prejudice, and grounds the church's salvation in the selfsame mercy of God which has been promised Israel."[24]

Interpretation

Why read the Bible? The answers supplied from earlier epochs are obvious: We read the Bible because it contains information of various sorts that is useful to humankind. For biblical texts to become useful, they must be understood and interpreted in theological, historical, or existential terms. The presupposition that biblical texts have such meanings that can be loosened from the ancient languages and forms and set forward for modern readers in contemporary idiom is compelling. Our libraries are filled with linguistico-historical commentaries, theological syntheses, and homiletic applications that offer the meaning and significance of biblical texts.

A different presupposition operates in the transformation of biblical texts into art and music, as well as into poetry and drama. It seems that a different world view is operative in art than in interpretation. In the biblical period itself, we have a creative telling and a retelling of the biblical stories, which is supported by an artistic or poetic perspective.

The easy supposition that the proper use of the Bible is its interpretation may be questioned not only from the early history of the reception and use of the Bible but also from contemporary developments. It could be argued that the failure to arrive at universally accepted interpretations—theological and historical—has caused us to move away from the attempt. Plurality of meaning and significance of biblical texts seems to belie assumptions of meaning that have guided us in biblical studies. But the conventional task of interpretation is also called into question by our rediscovery of the literary nature of the Bible. Are commentary and interpretation appropriate? If not, how do we make sense of the Bible today? If so, what sort of commentary and interpretation is appropriate for the Bible approached as literature?

Interpretation and the Uses of Language. The problem of interpretation may be illuminated by the variation in the validity and method of interpretation in different stages of language. In the first, or poetic, stage, the articulating of words was able to bring into being the power common to subject and object. These words of power are not to be argued about but are to "be accepted and pondered, their power absorbed by a disciple or reader" (*TGC*, p. 7). With the second, or metonymic, phase, which began with Plato, words become primarily the outward expression of inner thoughts or ideas. Interpretation, then, becomes possible, but the interpretation is governed not by the world view of the first stage but by that of the second stage.

> All through the metonymic period we have a tradition of commentary on myth informed by the general principle that a story-myth can carry a great number of "interpretations" or "meanings." Every example illustrates any number of precepts, just as any precept can be the moral of a fable. Major Classical poets, notably Homer and Virgil, came to be regarded as inexhaustible treasure-troves of metonymic ideas. Even Francis Bacon wrote a treatise on the "Wisdom of the Ancients," in which most of the standard Classical myths turned out to be prototypes of the principles of Baconian philosophy. (*TGC*, pp. 65-66)

The Bible was understood and interpreted within the same Platonic world view as other literature; acceptable meanings were confined to dogmatic statements. The Bible and the dogma of the Church could be set side by side and found to be saying the same thing by means of strategies of typology and allegory.

In the descriptive phase of language (which we take to be normative), the meaning sought was governed by the world view emphasized in science and mathematics. The critical study of the Bible emphasized statements that could be made consistent with various critical approaches by means of historical and critical strategies. The need for a conceptual language satisfying to the modern person reflects the world view of the descriptive stage.

> We ourselves live in a post-mythical age. . . . With the rise of science, the background of presuppositions on which mythical discourse proceeded has been gradually destroyed. Thus modern man finds that myth does not communicate to him, for the condition that language may communicate is precisely that one shares a frame of reference with the person who uses the language.[25]

Reading and Interpretation. The incompatibility of descriptive language and the message of the Bible presents a dilemma that may at least be relieved by contemporary satisfaction with approaches and meanings that are not designed to reduce the Bible to descriptive and objective truth. The view that the act of reading is to be seen as an end in itself seems to be an attempt in literature to return to an earlier stage of language.[26]

Poetry has kept alive the metaphorical use of language even in the scientific descriptive phase. Our approach to the Bible as poetry, then, may allow us to recover its message. In contemporary use of poetry, however, the original sense of magic disappears. No longer is there the idea of the possible forces being released by words of power. This does not mean that poetry really loses its magical power. The power is transferred "from an action on nature to an action on the reader or hearer" (*TGC*, p. 25). This may be particularly appropriate for biblical material, whose literary aspects are coordinated with a rhetorical function. It has been suggested, in fact, that the genre of the

Bible as a whole is that of proclamation, a mode of rhetoric.[27]

Our reading in a postmodern age is not precritical or uncritical. We return to a poetic stage after having experienced the descriptive stage of language. We remain entangled with the critical, even though it is relativized.

> It may be that in the end, after such an interpretation [in a conceptual language satisfying to modern man] has been offered, one can go back to the myth with a new appreciation. Certainly, one's attitude will be different from that of the archaic mentality that lived in the as yet undifferentiated myth, for now one recognizes the myth as myth. Yet, if an interpretive key has been found, the dramatic form of the myth may be found to communicate its insights with a forcefulness that would not belong to an abstract language.[28]

Actualizing the Reader of Biblical Texts

In the process of reading biblical literature, the reader is affected in the same fashion as are readers of all literature. There is intellectual and emotional pleasure as readers are able to analyze and synthesize the text as on the various levels. The intellectual pleasure of applying a limited number of codes becomes a more sensuous pleasure with the multiplication of codes. But biblical literature is different from other literature as it reveals a transcendent world and induces or "traps" readers to become a part of that world. The reader is trapped both by the tortuous sense-making experience required of some biblical texts and in the superior position of knowledge granted by other biblical texts. The completion of the only partially depicted world of the text and the imaginative actualization of a world presupposed by the text also play an important part. Most important, perhaps, is the creation and recreation of the world of the reader in the process of reading.

The Reader Trapped by Ignorance and Knowledge

Paratactic thinking on the various levels requires readers to come to some decision that is not made clear in the text itself. The two phrases of a sentence, the two lines of a poem, the two elements in the figurative expression, the paradoxical ideas in the narrative or teaching, all require mediation and completion by a reader. A reader cannot be passive or remain neutral. In making sense of stories such as those about Samson, Gideon, and Jonah, moreover, the reader is required to formulate hypotheses that must be reevaluated radically in the light of later information. The recognition of what is involved in making sense, as well as the result of the acts of making sense, is a part of the process of the actualization of the reader. If the literature were opaque with no complication, the reader would be able to treat the information obtained with equanimity, rejecting or accepting as the information conformed with the experience and knowledge of the reader or not.

> The combination of initial blurring and retrospective lucidity demonstrates to the reader, in terms of his own sense-making experience, the force of the generalization that 'man sees what meets the eye and God sees into the heart.' The world and its management are intelligible, but only to observers properly intelligent. (*PBN*, p. 99)

Sternberg emphasizes the enlightenment of the reader in the process of reading biblical literature. He speaks of "the tortuous route to enlightenment" and the way that the Bible goes out of its way to produce "curiosity," "wonder," and even "skepticism about God's disposition" as strategies that have the result of trapping readers into "faith on the backswing." (See *PBN,* p. 99.)

Biblical texts also operate so as to trap readers by their knowledge. In this strategy, readers are put in a privileged position so that they know what the characters in the stories do not know. When we read Nathan's story of the poor man with "nothing but one little ewe lamb," which is taken by a rich and selfish man, we know that David is that man. When David declares that "the man who has done this deserves to die," our knowledge and David's lack of knowledge produce rich irony. We are placed in Nathan's camp by the very composition. As suggested earlier, the Gospel of Mark is designed to capture the reader through this same sort of irony. The reader knows from the beginning what the disciples never seem to learn (by means of the initial biblical quotation in which God declares that he is sending his messenger to prepare the way of the Lord and by means of the voice at Jesus' baptism, declaring, "Thou art my beloved Son with thee I am well pleased"). It is instructive to attempt to relate all of the aspects of Mark mentioned earlier by means of the literary device of irony. The most famous moment of irony in Mark, of course, is the scene at the crucifixion, where bystanders mock and jeer at Jesus as he hangs on the cross. They say: "He saved others; he cannot save himself. Let the

Christ, the King of Israel, come down now from the cross, that we may see and believe." Irony here is operating at several levels. The mockers use ironic words when they call Jesus the Christ, the king of Israel. They do not mean that! But in the world of Mark, the words are true. Jesus is the Christ, The king of Israel. Against the background of information readers possess, they perceive the different levels of irony. But they also interpret actions and sayings of characters throughout the story as ironic. "The reader knows simultaneously that Jesus is the messiah and that this messiahship is hidden or obscured from characters in the story. That incongruity between what the reader knows and what the characters in the story know is the essence of irony."[29]

When the reader sees through the irony and perceives the genuine beliefs and judgments of the author, the reader will congratulate himself or herself on being perceptive without realizing the subtleness of the text and the process whereby the text encourages agreement with the values being expressed.

If Mark had presented us with a straight-forward religious tract, with simple, direct sentences declaring bluntly who Jesus is, many prospective readers would draw back and flee. But by indirect means, through constant use of irony, he is able, subtly and intriguingly, to portray a man who was despised, misunderstood, betrayed, and killed—someone for whom anyone reading Mark's Gospel invariably holds a certain amount of respect, sympathy, and admiration. And following respect, sympathy, and adoration may come allegiance and devotion.[30]

The Reader's Creation of Worlds of the Text

Readers who do not wish to treat the text as a shell to be thrown away after securing from it some factual information, but who wish to enjoy the richness and potentiality of the text, may go beyond an actualization of the text itself to an actualization of the worlds of the text. In such a process, filling in the gaps of language and logic is just a beginning. The text only *represents* characters, events, environment, and so on. (No text, for example, can present characters in their fullness!) An indeterminacy (or gap) exists in so far as each of the elements of the textual world and that world as a whole are concerned. Readers may make the represented persons, things, events, states and acts performed by persons less indeterminate by viewing the objects and their relationships from different perspectives and by supplying details omitted by the text. In the process, readers "gain a certain power over represented objects by influencing their constitution."[31] Readers vary in their need for and power of imaginative actualization of such things as characters and events in texts, and critics vary in their estimation of its value. Roman Ingarden, for example, emphasizes the filling in of "places of indeterminacy" as a major factor in reading. He indicates that "if a story talks about the fate of a very old man but does not say what color hair he has, then, theoretically, he can be given any color hair in the concretization." Wolfgang Iser takes the position that "the mental image of the old man can be just as concrete without our giving him grey hair." The reason for this is that (as a rule) "the presentation of facts in literary texts is of interest only in relation to their function: the extreme age of the old man is of no significance until it is connected to other facts or situations."[32] Readers concerned with the logic and ideology of the text may make such elements only as determinate as needed to make sense of the movement of the text. Others may need to "see" the environment, characters, and so on more fully than they are represented.

Disagreement over the need for more vivid actualization of the world represented in the text does not lead to a disagreement on the need for actualization of a world disclosed by the text. In Iser's opinion, the true communicatory function of literature lies in the reader's formulation of the cause underlying the questioning of the world in the text. The reader transcends the world of the text to formulate the unformulated background to which the formulations of the text refer. Beyond the linguistic and literary strata of the text, Ingarden sees a core of the literary work, which consists of qualities revealing a deeper sense of life and existence—and even *constituting* this usually hidden sense of life. Ingarden speaks of these metaphysical qualities as being revealed because they cannot be grasped as one grasps a mathematical theory. They allow themselves to be seen in the specific situations in which they are realized.

The world uncovered or revealed by the biblical text is a world that is not created or essentially sustained by human will and effort. It is a world properly spoken of as a given, or a gift, that parallels the world of the achievements of humankind. The world of the sacred and the world of the secular are both aspects of a mythological universe within which humans live together. Readers are not aware of the implications of reading literature from the perspective of the creation of a world of meaning, as children are largely unaware of the important value and role that play has in their lives. It is only long after the fact that we recognize the vital function of our adolescent play, and it may be after the fact that we become aware of the creation of a mythological universe in our reading.

The Reader's World

In the reading process, we somewhat automatically assume the perspective of the literary work. We enter the world of the narrative text, and we are carried along unconsciously as we establish the cause-and-effect relationships and relate the characters to the action. We enter, more consciously perhaps, into the didactic-rhetoric of non-narrative material in order to understand and appreciate the argumentation. The reader is able to make sense of the world of the text because there is not total discontinuity between the two worlds. We are aware of the necessity of interpreting the text from the perspective of the real world as the reader perceives it. The methodological assumption, however, is that the reader's world is ontologically "real" and is not itself an object of actualization.

In the clash of worlds at the level of ideology, the reader's world may become an object of actualization. In making sense of the stories of Israel and of Jesus, certain ideological aspects of the world of the text must be actualized by the reader. The reader whose world has been framed by experience (including the experience of literature) who sees the world essentially as a human quest is jolted by the picture of the world as a gracious gift. Those who share the biblical tradition of the sacrality of the world do not agree on all ideological assumptions and expressions of that world. The differences between the biblical ideologies of *Nomos,* prophecy, *Ethos,* and *Mythos* have been mentioned. A major difference (within broader agreement) exists between the ideological world of the Hebrew writings and that of the Christian writings. Even a sympathetic Jewish reader of the Gospels, for example, would have trouble with the messianism of what the reader would consider a post-biblical movement. "The kingdom of heaven (the 'Days of the Messiah')," declared Joseph Klausner, "is not yet come." This kingdom is "the sovereignty of good—worldly, material good as well as higher, spiritual good, for 'there is none good but one, and that is God.' " To the Jewish nation, Jesus cannot be the Messiah even though he is *"a great teacher of morality and an artist in parable."*[33] Klausner may have understood the convictions supporting the world of the Gospels better than those who unconsciously accept those convictions. Indeed, it is when a clash takes place that a reader becomes aware that ideological presupposition must be actualized to make sense of the text.

The reader's world may not only be challenged by the text, but it may also be changed. A major role of literature in general is to enable readers (and readership) to create a world or worlds for themselves, cognitively, affectively, behaviorally—

in all of the ways that individuals and groups are related to their world. At implicit and explicit levels, readers create their own worlds in the process of reading. World and self do not exist in isolation, however, and the reader is transformed in the process. Biblical texts share in this role in a particular way; they provide resources for the creation of a comprehensive universe, which has space for the human and for the divine and which sees the human in the light of the divine and the divine in the light of the human.

The clearly didactic purpose of some biblical texts may have a bearing on the dual function of the reader's creation of self and the ideological creation of the reader's world. Although biblical writings in general may be read as literature, some may be related more closely to didactic and propagandistic literature, whose purpose is "to communicate . . . a confirmation of values already known to the public." Such literature attempts to stabilize the system, and only if the values being protected are disputed in the reader's world is the communication meaningful as literature. In the case of didactic and propagandistic literature, the use of imagination in the concretization of the text is reduced. The thesis novel is an example. In such a novel, the subject matter is presented "as if it were a given object, and so the problem is merely to ensure the reliable communication of the thesis." This means that the contents must be linked closely to the expectations and dispositions of readers. With such literature, then, the reader participates not in the articulation of a specific meaning but in the articulation of "the reader's own situation *vis-a-vis* that meaning."[34] Biblical texts with obviously didactic purposes, as didactic literature in general, may engage readers more in the definition of their own ideological stance than to discovering the ideological significance of the text.

Conclusion: Wording the Wound of Words

Readers make sense of the Bible in the light of their world by means of methods supplied and validated by that world. A "fit" takes place, which involves such interdependent factors as the code of the natural language and supplementary literary codes, the sociological and historical circumstances of the text's origin, the conception of the role and function of biblical literature, and the psychological "set" and symbolic competence of the reader.

This volume advocates a hermeneutic reader-oriented literary approach to the Bible. From such a perspective, discovery and explication of factual scientific information about the history of the peoples involved with the Bible and with their religious and social convictions and traditions does not constitute the end of biblical study. Nor is the end of Bible study the discovery and display of dogmatic truth. (It is clear, of course, that the total field of critical study of the Bible includes many areas, and the end of many studies as scientific studies is the answering of limited scientific questions. The answering of these limited questions ought not to be confused with the answering of questions raised by readers of the Bible as literature.)

The perception that the end of biblical study is not the sort of information the critical approach supplies parallels the postmodern discovery of limitations (albeit the necessity) of the critical tradition. Because of the value and success of the critical tradition, it is tempting to engage in refutation of the postmodern assertions of the partiality of knowledge. It may be more profitable, however, to reconsider the role and function of the Bible and the relationship between the cognitive and the recognitive (the affective and volitional) functions of biblical literature.

Geoffrey Hartman has contrasted the cognitive and recognitive functions of literature in general and has shown the necessary relationship between the two functions. He has done this in the context of deconstruction's demonstration of the inability of language to present fully what it represents.

Hartman acknowledges the limitation of language, asserting even that words "wound" because we expect too much from them and search for the absolute word. (This is the cognitive function.) But he finds that literature has a "medicinal function," which is "to word a wound words have made." Words themselves help us tolerate the normal condition of "partial knowledge," which is the condition of living in the context of words. (This is the recognition function.) To confuse the cognitive and the recognitive is to miss the value of literature.

> To put the entire emphasis on the cognitive function . . . will damage the recognitive function . . . and the language exchange as a whole. Values continue to be created that may seem purely ritual, or not entirely perspicuous. Even when art represents a movement from ignorance to knowledge, it is not for the sake of

clearing up a simple misunderstanding or emending the human mind in an absolute manner.[35]

In so far as the cognitive is concerned, no text or group of texts can achieve the end of absolute knowledge or closure. Closure is possible, however, on the affective level. The relationship of affective volitional closure to the cognitive may be appreciated by attention to Stanley Cavell's observation that empirical statements are those that claim truth and depend on evidence, while truthful statements are those that claim truthfulness and depend on our acceptance of them. A true statement is something we know or do not know; a truthful statement, on the other hand, is one we acknowledge or fail to acknowledge. Acknowledgment is the "recognition" beyond cognition, which brings closure and the healing of the wounded spirit.[36]

Hartman denies that we can get beyond words. Words (threatening by their nature) must be heeded. But they need not be taken literally; life need not be lived under their sway. The closure of figurative action substitutes another meaning for the dread words, but this action constitutes "another set of words." "Words have been found which close the path to the original words. This absolute closure is what we respond to, this appearance of definitive detachment and substitution. The words themselves block the way. There is no going back, no stumbling through ghostly or psychoanalytic vaults: the 'dread Voice' exists as the poem or not at all."[37]

The biblical text shares the inability of the literary

text to present fully what it represents. The Bible as Word cannot be identified with the words; yet, there is a relationship. There must never be an easy identification, but there need be no divorce. The ultimacy of the Word and the temporality of the words reinforce and relativize each other. The experience of the reader and the actualization of biblical texts, then, may be seen in some sense as an experience of ultimacy. To be sure, this is not an experience that can bypass the historical and contingent. It is not an identification of the divine with the text; it is not even a deification of pure experience. It grows out of the recognition that *for us* in our pilgrimage deity *exists* in our imagining and imaginative constructs—or not at all.

In the reader centered approach, the *conceptualization* of ultimacy will be seen as an effect, the result of the imaginative work of readers in front of texts. Nevertheless the believer is no less able to claim a relationship of the imaginative construction to reality than is the historian, sociologist, or others who attribute reality to their abstractions. Is the image created by the believer less valid even than the hypothesis of the scientist who recognizes the partiality but validity of his hypothesis? It may be that the reader's construction of the divine in the process of making sense of text and world is, in fact, a more satisfying conceptualization of God than that in more dogmatic views. Deity is viewed not as "God is in Himself," not as the "unmoved mover," nor as other forms in which God is some static force essentially unrelated to world and humans. God is defined in terms of dynamic relationship—just as self and world.

In the present context of literary and biblical study, we seem to be able to appreciate the metaphorical or poetic use of language, even though we still operate against the horizon, or even within the formal constraints, of critical descriptive. We are not only able to turn to earlier functions of biblical literature from experiences in conceptual language and thought (as Macquarrie suggests) but we are also able to turn to conceptual language and thought from the *experience* of the Bible as literature. We may relate the biblical material to our lives by retelling, by transformation into the various artistic forms, by preaching, or by fitting the Bible into theological conceptualizations. When we move to conceptual language after the experience of literature, however, that language has changed its force. It is relativized. The interpretation we do in a contemporary context will be seen as the translation or recording of aspects of meaning uncovered in an experience of the reader into some sort of language and conceptuality shared by a community of contemporaries. Such language and conceptuality will not be able to contain all of the potential meanings or even all of the meanings possible in terms of the given language that is selected.

Notes

1. Umberto Eco, *A Theory of Semiotics* (Bloomington: Indiana University Press, 1976), p. 133. See also Eco, *The Role of the Reader: Explorations in the Semiotics of Texts* (Bloomington: Indiana University Press, 1979), pp. 19-20.

2. "Report of the Peace C•mmittee," *SBC Today* 5 (1987):11.

3. G. B. Caird, *The Language and Imagery of the Bible* (Philadelphia: The Westminster Press, 1980), p. 119.

4. Caird notes that in his ICC commentary C. A. Briggs "excises v. 3 as a pedantic gloss, though the pedantry is wholly his own" (Caird, *The Language and Imagery of the Bible,* p. 119).

5. James L. Kugel, *The Idea of Biblical Poetry: Parallelism and Its History* (New Haven, Conn.: Yale University Press, 1981), p. 10.

6. Proverbs 26:9 is cited by Kugel to illustrate the point: "A thorn comes by chance into the hand of a drunkard and a proverb [masal] into the mouth of fools." Kugel says the sense of the verse is that "you may hear fools citing words of wisdom, but they have gotten them without understanding their real meaning, by chance, like a burr that sticks into the hand of a groping drunkard." The image of the thorn is significant. A proverb (or a parallelistic line) is associated with something sharp, just as in Ecclesiastes 12:11. (Kugel, *The Idea of Biblical Poetry,* pp. 10-12.)

7. Caird, *The Language and Imagery of the Bible,* p. 121.

8. Ibid., p. 118.

9. Max Black, "Metaphor," *Proceedings of the Aristotelian Society* NS 55 (1954-55):293.

10. Amos N. Wilder set the stage for a thoroughgoing literary approach to the parables in 1964 in his *Early Christian Rhetoric: The Language of the Gospel*, rev. ed. (Cambridge, Mass.: Harvard University Press, 1971). For Wilder, the parable is an extended metaphor: "Now we know that a true metaphor or symbol is more than a sign, it is a bearer of the reality of which it refers. The hearer not only learns about that reality, he participates in it" (p. 84). Robert W. Funk followed Wilder's lead in 1966 with his *Language, Hermeneutics and the Word of God* (New York: Harper, 1966). Through the parable, the listener is led "into a strange world where everything is familiar yet radically different." This takes place through a "turn" in parables "which looks through the commonplace to a new view of reality. This 'turn' may be overt in the form of a surprising development in the narrative, an extravagant exaggeration, a paradox; or it may lurk below the surface in the so-called transference of judgment for which the parable calls" (p. 161). Other early attempts to use literary criticism to interpret the

parables so that they have contemporary relevance were those of Dan O. Via, Jr. (*The Parables: Their Literary and Existential Dimension*, [Philadelphia: Fortress Press, 1967]) and John Dominic Crossan (In *Parables: The Challenge of the Historical Jesus* [New York: Harper, 1973]). Norman Perrin was influenced by all of these scholars in his movement to a view of the kingdom as a symbol. "If 'Kingdom of God' is a 'steno-symbol' or 'sign' in the historical proclamation of Jesus, then our hermeneutical responsibility is earnestly to look for signs of the end and busily to calculate dates for the coming of the Son of Man. But if it is a 'tensive' or 'true' symbol, then our responsibility is to explore the manifold ways in which the experience of God can become an existential reality to man" (Perrin, "Eschatology and Hermeneutics: Reflections of Method in the Interpretation of the New Testament," *Journal of Biblical Literature* 93 [1974]:13).

11. *The New Oxford Annotated Bible with the Apocrypha*, p. 304, note on Judges 8:18-19.

12. It is this critical and volitional determination of the textual topic that "helps the reader to select the right frames, to reduce them to a manageable format, to blow up and to narcotize given semantic properties of the lexemes to be amalgamated, and to establish the isotopy according to which he decides to interpret the linear text manifestation so as to actualize the discoursive structure of a text" (Umberto Eco, *The Role of the Reader: Explorations in the Semiotics of Texts* [Bloomington: Indiana University Press, 1979], p. 27).

13. Wolfgang Iser, *The Act of Reading: A Theory of Aesthetic Response* (London: Routledge & Kegan Paul, 1978), p. 198.

14. Ibid., pp. 10, 37.

15. Wolfgang Iser, "The Reading Process: A Phenomenological Approach." In *Reader-Response Criticism: From Formalism to Post-Structuralism*, ed. Jane P. Tompkins (Baltimore: The Johns Hopkins University Press, 1980), p. 129. Reprinted from Wolfgang Iser, *The Implied Reader: Patterns in Communication in Prose Fiction from Bunyan to Beckett* (Baltimore: The Johns Hopkins University Press, 1974).

16. The term *genre* has been used to signify types of writings at different levels. Form criticism has generally dealt

with smaller units, such as legend, hymn, curse, lament, apothegm, and so on. At times the term *genre* is used to designate the character of larger literary units, such as historical and prophetic writings, epistle, apocalypse, gospel, and so on. The principle discussed here is applicable for genre at all levels.

17. James Kugel, "On the Bible and Literary Criticism," *Prooftexts: A Journal of Jewish Literary History* 1 (1981):219.

18. E. D. Hirsch, Jr. *Validity in Interpretation* (New Haven, Conn.: Yale University Press, 1967), pp. 53-54, 265.

19. Ibid., pp. 242-43.

20. Determinacy of meaning was conceived of by Hirsch, in his 1967 volume *Validity in Interpretation*, as a result of the author's will. Verbal meaning is what an author wills to convey by a sequence of linguistic signs. Later, of course, Hirsch moved to a concept of meaning that emphasizes the reader in his admission that "the nature of a text is to mean whatever we construe it to mean. . . . We, not our texts, are the makers of the meanings we understand, a text being only an occasion for meaning, in itself an ambiguous form devoid of the consciousness where meaning abides" (E. D. Hirsch, Jr., *The Aims of Interpretation* [Chicago: The University of Chicago Press, 1976], pp. 75-76).

21. Ernst Käsemann, "Justification and Salvation History in the Epistle to the Romans," in *Perspectives on Paul* (Philadelphia: Fortress Press, 1971), p. 72. The history-of-salvation approach of Krister Stendahl (see "The Apostle Paul and the Introspective Conscience of the West") effectively avoids the intellectual and religious embarrassment of a direct and naive application of Paul's statements to contemporary religious life, but such a hermeneutic may do less than full justice to the particulars of Paul's situation and communication.

22. Brevard S. Childs, *The New Testament as Canon: An Introduction* (Philadelphia: Fortress Press, 1984), p. 260.

23. Ibid., pp. 260-61.

24. Ibid.

25. John Macquarrie, *Principles of Christian Theology* (New

York: Charles Scribner's Sons, 1966), p. 120. Macquarrie indicates that if the insights of biblical languages are to be elicited "a new act of interpretation is called for, so that the insights of the myth can be expressed in a language that can communicate in a post-mythical world."

26. Frye suggests that poetry itself has the task "to keep re-creating the first or metaphorical phase of language during the domination of the later phases, to keep presenting it to us as a mode of language that we must never be allowed to underestimate, much less loose sight of" (*TGC*, p. 23). During the second phase, poetry recreated the metaphorical phase of language through the use of allegory. In Dante, for example, a metaphorical narrative runs parallel with a conceptual one. The metaphorical narrative, however, defers to the conceptual narrative. The poet would not be given the authority accorded the theologian and the sources of the conceptual side of Dante's allegory. In the third phase, literature utilized realism, "adopting categories of probability and plausibility as rhetorical devices." Zola is cited as a fairly extreme example. His novels have an obvious relation to sociology. In these novels, "the sociological aspect by definition is a more direct rendering of 'truth' than the fictional one." In the third stage, "the fictional mode is adopted because it presents a unity to the imagination more intense than the documentary materials. (See *TGC*, p. 25.)

27. "It is, like all rhetoric, a mixture of the metaphorical and the 'existential' or concerned but, unlike practically all other forms of rhetoric, it is not an argument disguised by figuration. It is the vehicle of what is traditionally called revelation, a word I use because it is traditional and I can think of no better one" (*TGC*, p. 29).

28. Macquarrie, *Principles of Christian Theology*, p. 120.

29. Robert Fowler, "Irony and the Messianic Secret in the Gospel of Mark," *Proceedings: Eastern Great Lakes Biblical Society* 1 (1981):29.

30. Ibid., p. 33.

31. Roman Ingarden, *The Literary Work of Art: An Investigation on the Borderlines of Ontology, Logic, and Theory of*

Literature, trans. George G. Grabowicz, Northwestern Studies in Phenomenology and Existential Philosophy (Evanston, Ill.: Northwestern University Press, 1973), p. 276.

32. Iser, *The Act of Reading*, pp. 176-77. Although Iser follows in the phenomenological tradition of Ingarden, he disagrees with the assumptions of Ingarden. "The implication is that a concretization must produce the object in such a way that it gives at least the illusion of a perception. This illusion, however, is just one paradigmatic instance of image-building and is in no way identifiable with the whole process of ideation" (Iser, *The Act of Reading*, pp. 176-77).

33. Joseph Klausner, *Jesus of Nazareth* (New York: Macmillan, 1925), pp. 414, 398.

34. Iser, *The Act of Reading*, pp. 83, 190.

35. Geoffrey H. Hartman, *Saving the Text: Literature/Derrida/Philosophy* (Baltimore: The Johns Hopkins University Press, 1981), pp. 131, 133, 134, 137. Paul de Man finds a performative aspect of language and text that is immune from deconstruction. As a figural system, the grammatical code to which the text owes its existence is subverted by a "transcendental signification" (Paul de Man, *Allegories of Reading: Figural Language in Rousseau, Nietzsche, Rilke, and Proust* [New Haven, Conn.: Yale University Press, 1979], p. 131).

36. The truth that depends on evidence and the truthfulness that involves acknowledgment and recognition cannot be divorced. The entanglement of the critical in the poetic is evidenced in Hartman's admission that the very desire manifested in his essay is an "aesthetic" manuver to master the fear of the equivocal nature of words by converting it into the will "to establish the ideal of science as pure cognition or disinterested knowledge." Knowledge desired in the form of *theoria* or *imitatio* is also pleasurable. The quietus sought in logic subverts logic itself (*Saving the Text*, p. 157).

37. Ibid.

Works Cited

Abrams, M. H. *The Mirror and the Lamp: Romantic Theory and the Critical Tradition*. New York: W. W. Norton, 1958.

Alter, Robert. *The Art of Biblical Narrative*. New York: Basic Books 1981.

Augustine, St. *On the Catechising of the Uninstructed*. A Select Library of the Nicene and Post-Nicene Fathers of the Christian Church, vol. 3, edited by Philip Schaff. Grand Rapids, Mich.: Wm. B. Eerdman's, 1956.

———. *On Christian Doctrine*. A Select Library of the Nicene and Post-Nicene Fathers of the Christian Church, vol. 2, edited by Philip Schaff. Grand Rapids, Mich: Wm. B. Eerdman's, 1956.

Barr, James. "Revelation Through History in the Old Testament and in Modern Theology." *Interpretation* 17 (1963):193-205.

Berger, Peter L. *A Rumor of Angels: Modern Society and the Rediscovery of the Supernatural*. Garden City, N.Y.: Anchor Books, 1970.

Black, Max. "Metaphor." *Proceedings of the Aristotelian Society* NS 55 (1954–55):273-94.

Bonner, Gerald. "Augustine as Biblical Scholar." In *From The Beginnings to Jerome*. The Cambridge History of the Bible, vol. 1: edited by P. R.

Ackroyd and C. F. Evans. Cambridge: Cambridge University Press, 1970.
———. *St. Augustine of Hippo: Life and Controversies.* The Library of History and Doctrine. Philadelphia: The Westminster Press, 1963.
Brown, Peter. *Augustine of Hippo.* Berkeley: University of California Press, 1967.
Bultmann, Rudolf. "Bultmann Replies to His Critics." In *Kerygma and Myth,* vol. 1, edited by Hans Werner Bartsch. New York: Harper Torchbooks, 1961.
———. *The History of the Synoptic Tradition,* translated by John Marsh. New York: Harper, 1963.
———. "The Primitive Christian Kerygma and the Historical Jesus." In *The Historical Jesus and the Kerygmatic Christ,* edited and translated by Carl E. Braaten and Roy A. Harrisville. Nashville: Abingdon Press, 1964.
———. "The Problem of Hermeneutics." In *Essays Philosophical and Theological,* translated by James C. Greig. London: SCM, 1955.

Caird, G. B. *The Language and Imagery of the Bible.* Philadelphia: The Westminster Press, 1980.
Childs, Brevard S. *The New Testament as Canon: An Introduction.* Philadelphia: Fortress Press, 1984.
———. *Introduction to the Old Testament as Scripture.* Philadelphia: Fortress Press, 1979.
Crossan, John Dominic. *In Parables: The Challenge of the Historical Jesus.* New York: Harper, 1973.

De Man, Paul. *Allegories of Reading: Figural Language in Rousseau, Nietzsche, Rilke, and Proust.* New Haven, Conn.: Yale University Press, 1979.

Derrida, Jacques. "Différance." In *Margins of Philosophy,* translated by Alan Bass. Chicago: The University of Chicago Press, 1982.

Dibelius, Martin. *From Tradition to Gospel.* Translated by Bertram Lee Woolf. New York: Charles Scribner's Sons, 1935.

Dijk, Teun A. Van. "Advice on Theoretical Poetics." *Poetics* 8 (1979):569-608

Dilthey, Wilhelm. *Gesammelte Schriften,*VII, 5th ed. Göttingen: Vandenhoeck & Ruprecht, 1968.

Dodd, C. H. *The Parables of the Kingdom.* New York: Charles Scribner's Sons, 1961.

Dreyfus, F. "Exégèse en Sorbonne, Exégèse en Eglise." *Revue Biblique* 81 (1975):321-59.

Eagleton, Terry. *Criticism and Ideology: A Study of Marxist Literary Theory.* London: New Left Books, 1976.

Ebeling, Gerhard, "Dogmatik und Exegese." *Zeitschrift für Theologie und Kirche* 77 (1980):269-86.

Eco, Umberto. *The Role of the Reader: Explorations in the Semiotics of Texts.* Bloomington, Ind.: Indiana University Press, 1979.

———. "A Semiotic Approach to Semantics." *Versus* 1 (1971):21-60.

———. *A Theory of Semiotics.* Bloomington: Indiana University Press, 1976.

Eliot, T. S. *The Use of Poetry and the Use of Criticism.* Cambridge, Mass.: Harvard University Press, 1933.

Fish, Stanley. *Is There a Text in This Class? The Authority of Interpretative Communities.* Cambridge, Mass.: Harvard University Press, 1980.

Fishbane, Michael. "The Notion of a Sacred Text." Paper delivered at Conference on "Sacred Texts," Indiana University, October 17-20, 1982.

Fosdick, Harry Emerson. *The Modern Use of the Bible.* New York: Macmillan, 1924.

Fowler, Robert M. "Irony and the Messianic Secret in the Gospel of Mark." *Proceedings: Eastern Great Lakes Biblical Society,* 1 (1981):26-36

Frye, Northrop. *Anatomy of Criticism: Four Essays.* Princeton, N.J.: Princeton University Press, 1957.

———. *The Great Code: The Bible and Literature.* New York: Harcourt Brace Jovanovich, 1982.

———. *The Secular Scripture: A Study of the Structure of Romance.* The Charles Eliot Norton Lectures, 1974–75. Cambridge, Mass.: Harvard University Press, 1976.

Funk, Robert W. *Language, Hermeneutics, and the Word of God: The Problem of Language in the New Testament and Contemporary Theology.* New York: Harper, 1966.

Geller, Stephen A. "Were the Prophets Poets?" *Prooftexts: A Journal of Jewish Literary History* 3 (1983):211-21.

Gottwald, Norman K. *The Hebrew Bible: A Socio-Literary Introduction.* Philadelphia: Fortress Press, 1985.

———. "Literary Criticism of the Hebrew Bible: Retrospect and Prospect."" Paper delivered to the Section on Biblical Criticism and Literary Criticism at the national meeting of the Society of Biblical Literature, November 24, 1986.

Goulder, M.D. *Type and History in Acts.* London: S.P.C.K., 1964.

Hartman, Geoffrey H. *Saving the Text: Literature/Derrida/Philosophy*. Baltimore: The Johns Hopkins University Press, 1981.

Harvey, Van Austin. *The Historian and the Believer: The Morality of Historical Knowledge and Christian Belief*. New York: Macmillan, 1966.

Hirsch, E. D., Jr. *The Aims of Interpretation*. Chicago: The University of Chicago Press, 1976.

———. *Validity in Interpretation*. New Haven, Conn.: Yale University Press, 1967.

Holland, Norman N. *The Dynamics of Literary Response*. Norton Library. New York: W. W. Norton & Company, 1968.

———. *Five Readers Reading*.New Haven, Conn.: Yale University Press, 1975.

Ingarden, Roman. *The Cognition of the Literary Work of Art*, translated by Ruth Ann Crowley and Kenneth R. Olson. Northwestern Studies in Phenomenology and Existential Philosophy. Evanston, Ill.: Northwestern University Press, 1973.

———. *The Literary Work of Art: An Investigation on the Borderlines of Ontology, Logic, and Theory of Literature*, translated by George G. Grabowicz. Northwestern Studies in Phenomenology and Existential Philosophy. Evanston, Ill.: Northwestern University Press, 1973.

Iser, Wolfgang. *The Act of Reading: A Theory of Aesthetic Response*. London: Routledge & Kegan Paul, 1978.

———. "The Reading Process: A Phenomenological Approach." In *Reader-Response Criticism: From Formalism to Post-Structuralism*, edited by Jane P.

Tompkins. Baltimore: The Johns Hopkins University Press, 1980. Reprinted from Wolfgang Iser, *The Implied Reader: Patterns in Communication in Prose Fiction from Bunyan to Beckett*. Baltimore: The Johns Hopkins University Press, 1974.

Jakobson, Roman. "Closing Statement: Linguistics and Poetics." In *Semiotics: An Introductory Anthology*, edited by Robert E. Innes. Bloomington: Indiana University Press, 1985.

Jameson, Fredric. *The Political Unconscious: Narratives as a Socially Symbolic Act*. Ithaca, N.Y.: Cornell University Press, 1981.

Jauß, Hans Robert. "Paradigmawechsel in der Literaturwissenschaft." *Linguistische Berichte* 3 (1969):44-56.

Jonas, Hans. *Gnosis und spätantiker Geist*, vol. 1. Göttingen: Vandenhoeck & Ruprecht, 1934.

Käsemann, Ernst. "Justification and Salvation History in the Epistle to the Romans." In *Perpsectives on Paul*. Philadelphia: Fortress Press, 1971.

Kelsey, David H. *The Uses of Scripture in Recent Theology*. Philadelphia: Fortress Press, 1975.

Klausner, Joseph. *Jesus of Nazareth*. New York: Macmillan, 1925.

Koester, Helmut. "New Testament Introduction: A Critique of a Discipline." In *Christianity, Judaism and Other Greco-Roman Cults: Studies for Morton Smith at Sixty*, Part One, New Testament. Leiden: E. J. Brill, 1975.

Kolakowski, Leszek. "Descartes, René." In *The*

Encyclopedia of Religion, vol. 4. New York: Macmillan, 1987.

Krausser, Peter. *Kritik der endlichen Vernunft:Wilhelm Diltheys Revolution der allgemeinen Wissenschafts- und Handlungstheorie.* Frankfurt: Suhrkamp Verlag, 1968.

Kugel, James L. *The Idea of Biblical Poetry: Parallelism and Its History.* New Haven, Conn.: Yale University Press, 1981.

———. "On the Bible and Literary Criticism." *Prooftexts: A Journal of Jewish Literary History* 1 (1981):217-36.

Levin, Samuel R., "On The Progress of Structural Poetics." *Poetics* 8 (1979):513-15.

Long, Eugene Thomas. *Existence, Being and God: An Introduction to the Philosophical Theology of John Macquarrie.* New York: Paragon House Publishers, 1985.

Lotman, Jurij. *Analysis of the Poetic Text,* edited and translated by D. Barton Johnson. Ann Arbor: Ardis, 1975.

———. "The Future for Structural Poetics." *Poetics* 8 (1979):501-7.

———. *The Structure of the Artistic Text.* Michigan Slavic Contributions 7, translated by Gail Lenhoff and Ronald Vroon. Ann Arbor: The University of Michigan, 1977.

Lowth, Robert. *Lectures on the Sacred Poetry of the Hebrews,* translated by G. Gregory. London: J. Johnson, 1878.

McCoy, Charles S. *When Gods Change: Hope for Theology.* Nashville: Abingdon Press, 1980.

McKnight Edgar V. *The Bible and the Reader: An*

Introduction to Literary Criticism. Philadelphia: Fortress press, 1985.

———. *Meaning in Texts: The Historical Shaping of a Narrative Hermeneutics*. Philadelphia: Fortress Press, 1978.

Macquarrie, John. *Principles of Christian Theology*. New York: Charles Scribner's Sons, 1966.

Marxsen, Willi. *Mark the Evangelist: Studies on the Redaction History of the Gospel*, translated by James Boyce et al. Nashville: Abingdon Press, 1969.

Matthews, Shailer. *The Faith of Modernism*. New York: Macmillan, 1924.

Mukarovsky, Jan. *Aesthetic Function, Norm and Value as Social Facts*. Ann Arbor: Department of Slavic Languages and Literature, University of Michigan, 1970.

———. "Intentionality and Unintentionality in Art." In *Structure, Sign, and Function: Selected Essays by Jan Mukarovsky*, edited and translated by John Burbank and Peter Steiner. New Haven, Conn.: Yale University Press, 1978.

———. "On Structuralism." In *Structure, Sign, and Function: Selected Essays by Jan Mukarovsky*, edited and translated by John Burbank and Peter Steiner. New Haven, Conn.: Yale University Press, 1978.

Payne, Ernest A. *The Fellowship of Believers: Baptist Thought and Practice Yesterday and Today*. London: The Carey Kingsgate Press, 1952.

Peirce, Charles Sanders. *Collected Papers*. Cambridge, Mass.: Harvard University Press, 1931-35.

Perrin, Norman. "Eschatology and Hermeneutics: Reflections on Method in the Interpretation of the

New Testament." *Journal of Biblical Literature* 93 (1974):3-14.

Richardson, Alan. "The Rise of Modern Biblical Scholarship and Recent Discussion of the Authority of the Bible." In "The West from the Reformation to the Present," vol. 3, In *The Cambridge History of the Bible,* S. L. Greenslade. Cambridge, England: Cambridge University Press, 1963.

Robertson, David. *The Old Testament and the Literary Critic.* Philadelphia: Fortress Press, 1977.

Robinson, James M. *A New Quest of the Historical Jesus.* London: SCM, 1959.

Rockmore, Tom. *Hegel's Circular Epistemology.* Bloomington: Indiana University Press, 1986.

Ryken, Leland. *How to Read the Bible as Literature.* Grand Rapids, Mich.: Academie Books.

Sanders, James A. *Canon and Community: A Guide to Canonical Criticism.* Guides to Biblical Scholarship. Philadelphia: Fortress press, 1984.

———. "Hermeneutics." In *The Interpreter's Dictionary of the Bible,* Supplementary Volume. Nashville: Abingdon Press, 1976.

———. *Torah and Canon.* Philadelphia: Fortress Press, 1972.

Saussure, Ferdinand de. *Course in General Linguistics,* rev. ed., edited by Charles Bally and Albert Sechehaye in collaboration with Albert Riedlinger, translated by Wade Baskin. London: Peter Owen, 1974.

Schlatter, Adolf. "Ätheistische Methoden in der Theologie." In *Zur Theologie des Neuen Testaments und zur Dogmatik: Kleine Schriften mit einer Einfuhrung*, edited by U. Luck. Munich: Chr. Kaiser Verlag, 1969.

———. *Das Christliche Dogma*, 2nd ed. Stuttgart: Calwer Verlag, 1923 (reprinted 1977).

Smith, Barbara Herrnstein. "Fixed Marks and Variable Constants: A Parable of Literary Value." *Poetics Today* 1 (1970):7-22.

Stendahl, Krister. "The Apostle Paul and the Introspective Conscience of the West." *Harvard Theological Review* 56 (1963):199-215.

———. "Contemporary Biblical Theology." In *The Interpreter's Dictionary of The Bible*, vol. 1. Nashville: Abingdon Press, 1962.

Sternberg, Meir. *The Poetics of Biblical Narrative: Ideological Literature and the Drama of Reading*. Bloomington: Indiana University Press, 1985.

Stuhlmacher, Peter. *Historical Criticism and Theological Interpretation of Scripture: Towards a Hermeneutics of Consent*, translated by Roy A. Harrisville. Philadelphia: Fortress Press, 1977.

———. *Vom Verstehen des Neuen Testament: Eine Hermeneutik*. Grundrisse zum Neuen Testament 6. Göttingen: Vandenhoeck & Ruprecht, 1st ed., 1979; 2nd ed., 1986.

Talmon, Shemaryahu. "The 'Comparative' Method in Biblical Interpretation—Principles and Problems." *Göttingen Congress Volume*. Leiden, 1978.

Tarski, Alfred. "The Semantic Conception of Truth." In *Readings in Philosophical Analysis*, edited by Herbert Feigl and Wilfrid Sellars. New York: Appleton-Century-Crofts, 1949.

Tracy, David. *Blessed Rage for Order: The New*

Pluralism in Theology. The Seabury Library of Contemporary Theology. New York: Seabury Press, 1979.

Troeltsch, Ernst. "Contingency." In *Encyclopedia of Religion and Ethics,* vol. 4, edited by James Hastings. New York: Charles Scribner's Sons, 1925.

———. "Historiography." In *Encyclopedia of Religion and Ethics,* vol. 6.

———. "Über historische und dogmatische Methode in der Theologie" (On Historical and Dogmatic Method in Theology). In *Gesammelte Schriften,* vol. 2. Tübingen: J. C. B. Mohr, 1913.

Vahanian, Gabriel. *The Death of God.* New York: George Braziller, 1961.

Via, Dan O., Jr. "A Quandry of Contemporary New Testament Scholarship: The Time Between the 'Bultmanns.'" *Journal of Religion* 55 (1975):456-61.

———. *The Parables: Their Literary and Existential Dimension.* Philadelphia: Fortress Press, 1967.

Vodicka, Felix. "Die Konkretisation des Literarischen Werks: Zur Problematik der Rezeption von Nerudas Werk." In *Die Struktur der Literarischen Entwicklung,* edited by Jurij Striedter. Munich: Wilhelm Fink, 1976.

Weinsheimer, Joel C. *Gadamer's Hermeneutics: A Reading of "Truth and Method."* New Haven, Conn.: Yale University Press, 1985.

Wellek, René. *Concepts of Criticism,* edited with an introduction by Stephen G. Nichols, Jr. New Haven, Conn.: Harcourt, Brace & Co., 1942.

Wellek, René and Austin Warren. *Theory of Literature*. New York: Harcourt, Brace & Co., 1942.

Wilder, Amos N. *Early Christian Rhetoric: The Language of the Gospel*, rev. ed. Cambridge, Mass.: Harvard University Press, 1971.

Winner, Thomas G. "The Aesthetics and Poetics of the Prague Linguistic Circle." *Poetics* 8 (1973).

Wood, Charles M. *The Formation of Christian Understanding: An Essay in Theological Hermeneutics*. Philadelphia: The Westminster Press, 1981.

INDEX OF AUTHORS

INDEX OF SCRIPTURE REFERENCES